knitted
nursery

TOYS, CLOTHES AND FURNISHINGS
FOR A BEAUTIFUL BABY'S ROOM

knitted
nursery

TOYS, CLOTHES AND FURNISHINGS
FOR A BEAUTIFUL BABY'S ROOM

Nancy Atkinson &
Sarah Jane Tavner

GUILD OF MASTER
CRAFTSMAN PUBLICATIONS

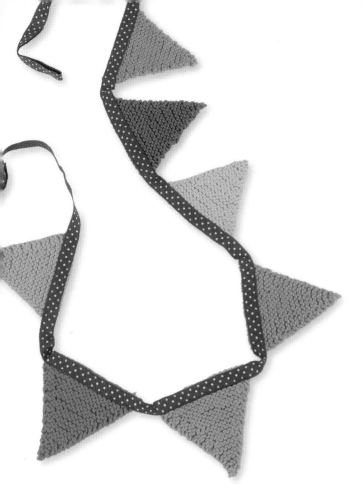

First published 2010 by
Guild of Master Craftsman Publications Ltd
Castle Place, 166 High Street, Lewes,
East Sussex BN7 1XU

Reprinted 2010

Text © Nancy Atkinson and Sarah Jane Tavner, 2010

© in the Work GMC Publications Ltd, 2010

ISBN: 978-1-86108-669-3

A catalogue record for this book is available from
the British Library.

Publisher: Jonathan Bailey
Production Manager: Jim Bulley
Managing Editor: Gerrie Purcell
Senior Project Editor: Virginia Brehaut
Editor: Robin Pridy
Managing Art Editor: Gilda Pacitti
Design: Rebecca Mothersole, JC Lanaway
Photography: Chris Gloag, Rebecca Mothersole

Colour origination by GMC Reprographics

Printed and bound in China by Hing Yip

Contents

Introduction

Preparing for a new arrival is a magical and exciting time. Whether it's your own baby, or the baby of a friend or relative, *Knitted Nursery* is a complete guide to creating a perfect, cozy, brightly coloured and, above all, unique space that can't be bought on the high street.

Individual style

These pages are bursting with original patterns to help you create a vibrant and stimulating environment, full of strong colours, shapes and bright contrasts, which babies and young children will love. The projects are simple and quick to make – whether you are a beginner or a more advanced knitter, they are achievable using just a few basic techniques.

How to use this book

The book is organized so that the simplest patterns come first and new techniques are introduced with each chapter. The patterns are labelled with symbols to show their difficulty (see below).

Beginners can work through the patterns in this book chronologically to build up their skills and achieve the more complex projects. Experienced knitters will find the patterns quick and satisfying. All of the designs are practical and portable as they are knitted in sections and need only a minimum of equipment – all of them require just one pair of 4mm (US6, UK8) needles and DK yarn.

At the back of the book you'll find a techniques chapter to help you through with step-by-step guides. The most important thing is to be creative – once you have mastered the basics, don't be afraid to embellish or adapt patterns to create a perfectly customized, bold and beautiful nursery.

Happy knitting!

Sarah Jane and Nancy

DIFFICULTY SYMBOLS

The simplest project for beginners or speedy knits for experienced knitters.

The pattern is simple but involves skills such as increasing and decreasing.

These patterns are still straightforward but bring more skills together at the same time.

Snuggly squares

Snuggle blanket

A baby blanket is a nursery essential. This gorgeous snuggle blanket is made of simple squares in vibrant cotton colours and has a handy button tie at the corner to keep it secured to the side of the cot or pram. It's the perfect project to start you off on the road to creating your very own knitted nursery. All the squares are the same size and you can choose your favourite colours to make a bold and personalized statement.

Yarns

Debbie Bliss Cotton DK

- ❧ Yellow (shade 35) 2 x 50g balls
- ❧ Red (shade 38) 2 x 50g balls
- ❧ Blue (shade 39) 1 x 50g ball
- ❧ Pale blue (shade 09) 1 x 50g ball
- ❧ Pale green (shade 20) 1 x 50g ball
- ❧ Bright green (shade 43) 1 x 50g ball
- ❧ Orange (shade 42) 1 x 50g ball
- ❧ Bright pink (shade 44) 1 x 50g ball

For the button tie:
You will need oddments, approx ¼ of a 50g ball. We have used Orange (shade 42) but you can use any colour you choose.

Tension

20 sts and 28 rows to 4in (10cm) square

Needles

1 pair 4mm (US6, UK8) needles

Other materials

- ❧ Darning needle
- ❧ 1 x 1½in (4cm) diameter plastic button in a contrasting colour to your yarn for the button tie

Snuggle blanket

Cast on 20 sts.
Work in garter stitch for 28 rows or until your work measures 4in (10cm).
Cast off.
Make 36 different-coloured squares (or 35 squares if you want to add a button tie to the corner of your blanket).

Button tie
Cast on 40 sts.
Rows 1–6: Knit.
Row 7 (buttonhole row): K4, cast off 4, k to end.
Row 8 (buttonhole row): K up to buttonhole, turn the work and cast on 4 sts, ensure that you pull the yarn very tight as you cast on. Turn the work back and k to end. (For additional technical help with buttonholes, see page 131.)
Rows 9–14: Knit.
Row 15 (decrease row): With right side facing you, cast off 20 sts. K to end (20 sts).
Continue to work in garter stitch for next 13 rows or until your work measures 4in (10cm). Cast off.

TOP TIP
This blanket is a good size for a newborn baby but you can continue to add to the blanket as the baby grows, or even make a larger version for grown-ups. Just knit extra squares and sew to the edge.

Making up

Lay out your 36 squares with their cast-on edge at the top. Jumble up the colours and sew up using mattress stitch. Using the darning needle, weave all your ends in. Sew your button very securely into place on the button tie. Ensure you knot the yarn at the back of the button several times for extra security. Sew your button tie to the corner of your blanket using mattress stitch.

Snuggle cushion cover

Create a comfy cushion with small patchwork squares – perfect for a nursery rocking chair or cozy story-telling corner. Choose as many or as few colours as you like or use up oddments of yarn left over from the snuggle blanket on page 12. The cover is fastened with buttons – so it's easy to remove and keep clean.

Yarns

Debbie Bliss Cotton DK
You will need oddments (approximately ¼ of a 50g ball) in eight colours of your choice. We have used:

Front:

- Yellow (shade 35)
- Red (shade 38)
- Blue (shade 39)
- Pale blue (shade 09)
- Pale green (shade 20)
- Bright green (shade 43)
- Orange (shade 42)
- Bright pink (shade 44)

Back:

- Orange (shade 42) 3 x 50g balls

Tension

20 sts and 28 rows to 4in (10cm) square

Needles

1 pair 4mm (US6, UK8) needles

Other materials

- Three 1½in (4cm) diameter plastic buttons in a contrasting colour to your yarn
- Cushion pad, 12 x 12in (30 x 30cm)
- Darning needle

Snuggle cushion cover

Front

Cast on 10 sts.
Work in garter stitch for 14 rows or until
your work measures 2in (5cm).
Cast off.
Make 36 squares.

Back

Piece 1

Cast on 60 sts.
Work in garter stitch for 33 rows or until
your work measures 5in (12cm).
Cast off.

Piece 2

Cast on 60 sts.
Rows 1–9: Knit.
Row 10 (buttonhole row): K10 sts, cast off
4 sts, k14 sts, cast off 4 sts, k14 sts, cast off 4,
k10 sts.
Row 11 (buttonhole row): K10 sts, turn work,
cast on 4 sts, turn work back, k14 sts, turn
work, cast on 4 sts, turn work back, k14 sts,
turn work, cast on 4 sts, turn work back,
k10 sts.
Work in garter stitch for 70 rows or until work
measures 10in (25cm).
Cast off.
(For additional technical help with
buttonholes, see page 131.)

TENSION ALERT!
Tension matters a little in this
pattern, as you want your cover
to fit the pillow pad. If you have
very loose tension or very tight
tension you might like to make
up the cushion cover first and then
buy a pad to fit. (See page 132 for
more information about tension
and when it matters.)

Making up
Front
Lay out your 36 squares with their cast-on edge at the top. Jumble up the colours and sew up using mattress stitch. Weave all your ends in. (See page 136 for technical help.)

Back
Sew your buttons very securely onto piece 1. Ensure that you knot the yarn at the back of the buttons several times for extra security. Sew piece 1 to the front piece of your cushion cover using mattress stitch. Sew piece 2 to your cushion cover, ensuring your buttonholes are in the right place. You should have an overlap between the pieces of around 2–2½in (5–6cm).

Cute cubes

ABC blocks

These ABC blocks look fantastic and are fun for a baby to stack up and knock down. The cubes couldn't be simpler and are made from the same square panels as the snuggle blanket on page 12. The base is a simple cube of furniture foam. It's as easy as A, B, C! You could even make more to spell out the baby's name.

Yarns
Debbie Bliss Cotton DK

Block A
- Yellow (shade 35) ½ x 50g ball
- Bright green (shade 43) ½ x 50g ball
- Blue (shade 39) ½ x 50g ball

Block B
- Yellow (shade 35) ½ x 50g ball
- Bright pink (shade 44) ½ x 50g ball
- Pale green (shade 20) ½ x 50g ball

Block C
- Red (shade 38) ½ x 50g ball
- Blue (shade 39) ½ x 50g ball
- Bright green (shade 43) ½ x 50g ball

Tension
20 sts and 28 rows to 4in (10cm) square

Needles
1 pair 4mm (US6, UK8) needles

Other materials
- Felt in three contrasting colours, we have used blue, yellow and red
- Fine-pointed needle and thread in matching colours for sewing the felt to your blocks
- Three cubes of fire-resistant furniture foam, 4 x 4in (10 x 10cm) – or, if you have very loose tension, have your foam cut after you have knitted your pieces for a perfect fit. Any good foam supplier should be able to cut you a piece to order. (See suppliers on page 141 for further information.)
- Darning needle

ABC blocks

Squares

Cast on 20 sts.
Work in garter stitch for 28 rows or
until your work measures 4in (10cm).
Cast off.
Make six squares for each cube
(two squares of each colour).

Felt

Trace or photocopy the felt letter templates
opposite. Cut the letters out and pin to felt.
Cut around the felt.

Templates for
ABC blocks
(shown at actual size)

TENSION ALERT!
So far in this book, the patterns have
not really required you to be too
accurate with your tension. Now that
you are starting to work with foam,
it's more important that you check
your tension or you could end up
knitting pieces that are too big or
small to fit your foam cubes. See page
132 for more information on tension.

Making up

Pin your knitted squares to your foam cube. Sew up using mattress stitch. Weave in your ends. Using straight stitch, sew your felt letters to your cube with a thread that matches the colour of your felt. (For more technical help on mattress and straight stitch, see page 136.)

TOP TIP
For more interactive ABC blocks, cut a slit in the foam and insert a bell or a toy squeaker.

Giant dice

Put your feet up with this gorgeous giant rollable dice! It's made from ruby-red cotton with contrasting felt circles over a simple foam cube. Straightforward but versatile, it's a stunning nursery footstool, a great toy and a brilliant teaching aid all in one – use it to help teach toddlers to count!

Yarns

Rowan Handknit Cotton DK
- Red (shade 215) 5 x 50g balls

Tension

19–20 sts and 28 rows to 4in (10cm) square

Needles

1 pair 4mm (US6, UK8) needles

Other materials

- Felt – we have used yellow, but you can use any contrasting colour of your choice
- Thread in matching colour for sewing spots onto your dice
- Fine-pointed needle for sewing felt to your dice
- Pins for pinning your work to the foam when making up
- One cube of fire-resistant furniture foam, 8 x 8in (20 x 20cm) – or if you have very loose tension, have your foam cut after you have knitted your pieces for a perfect fit. Any good foam supplier should be able to cut you a piece to order. (See suppliers on page 141 for further information.)
- Darning needle

Giant dice

Squares

Cast on 40 sts.
Work in garter stitch for 56 rows or until your work measures 8in (20cm).
Cast off.
Make 6 squares.

Felt

Trace or photocopy the felt dot template opposite. Cut the dots out and pin to felt. Cut around the felt.

Making up

Pin your knitted squares to your foam cube. Sew up using mattress stitch. Weave in your ends. Pin your felt dots in place. Using straight stitch, sew your felt dots to your cube with a thread that matches the colour of your felt. (For more technical help on mattress and straight stitch see page 136.)

TENSION ALERT!
This is a foam project, so it's more important that you check your tension, or you could end up knitting pieces that are too big or small to fit your foam cubes. See page 132 for information on tension.

Template
for dice dots
(shown at
actual size).

Lazy days armchair

This fabulous armchair is a haven for an older baby or toddler. The cover is made in simple panels and is removable for easy clean-up. The armchair base is constructed from pre-cut pieces of foam and glued using furniture glue. Unique, durable and practical, it's the perfect place for storytime!

Yarns
Debbie Bliss Cotton DK
- Yellow (shade 35) 5 x 50g balls
- Red (shade 38) 6 x 50g balls
- Pale green (shade 20) 5 x 50g balls
- Bright green (shade 43) 5 x 50g balls
- Bright pink (shade 44) 5 x 50g balls

Tension
20 sts and 28 rows to 4in (10cm) square

Needles
1 pair 4mm (US6, UK8) needles

Other materials
To construct the foam interior of the armchair you will need the following pieces of fire-resistant furniture foam:
- 12 x 12 x 12in (30 x 30 x 30cm) seat x 1
- 20 x 20 x 4in (50 x 50 x 10cm) back x 1
- 12 x 16 x 4in (30 x 40 x 10cm) arms x 2
- Foam or furniture glue
- Darning needle

Lazy days armchair

Top
(make 5, 1 in each colour)
Cast on 20 sts.
Work in garter stitch for 25 rows or until work measures 3½in (9cm).
Cast off.

Back rest
(make 1 yellow, 1 pale green and 1 bright green)
Cast on 20 sts.
Work in garter stitch until work measures 7½in (19cm).
Cast off.

Seat
(make 1 yellow, 1 pale green and 1 bright green)
Cast on 20 sts.
Work in garter stitch until work measures 11in (28cm).
Cast off.

Front
Section A (make 1 red and 1 pink)
Cast on 20 sts.
Work in garter stitch until work measures 15in (38cm).
Cast off.
Section B (make 1 pale green, 1 yellow and 1 bright green)
Cast on 20 sts.
Work in garter stitch until work measures 11in (28cm).
Cast off.

Arms
Tops (make 1 red and 1 pink)
Cast on 20 sts.
Work in garter stitch until work measures 11in (28cm).
Cast off.
Inside arm (make 1 yellow and 1 pale green)
Cast on 20 sts.
Work in garter stitch until work measures 11in (28cm).
Cast off.

Outer sides
Section A (make 1 pale green, 1 bright green, 2 yellow, 1 pink, and 1 red)
Cast on 20 sts.
Work in garter stitch until work measures 15in (38cm).
Cast off.
Section B (make 1 pale green and 1 bright green)
Work in garter stitch until work measures 19in (48cm).
Cast off.

Back
(make 5, 1 in each colour)
Cast on 20 sts.
Work in garter stitch until work measures 19in (48cm).
Cast off.

Bottom
Section A (make 2)
Cast on 20 sts in a colour of your choice.
Work in garter stitch until work measures 19in (48cm).
Cast off.
Section B (make 2)
Cast on 20 sts in a colour of your choice.
Work in garter stitch until work measures 7in (18cm).
Cast off.

TOP TIP
Take care to label your finished sections – front, back, side, etc – as you go along, to avoid a muddle when you come to sewing up at the end!

Making up

In a well-ventilated area, glue your foam pieces together to create your armchair 'shape'. Next, pin your knitted panels to your foam chair and sew them together using mattress stitch. Finally, turn the chair over and sew on your bottom strips to create a picture frame shape.

Using an oddment of yarn and a darning needle, sew a running stitch around the edge of your 'picture frame'. Pull the yarn tight and tie it in a bow. Your cover should fit the chair snugly and be removable for washing.

Top triangles

Cot bunting

This nostalgic bunting brings charm to any room and creates a colourful visual focus for a child. It's made using garter stitch and simple decrease stitches which combine to create the triangles. Be sure to use bold colours – perfect to string across the cot, changing table or door frame.

Yarns

Debbie Bliss Cotton DK
You will need oddments, (approx ¼ of a 50g ball) in six colours of your choice. We have used:

- 🌀 Blue (shade 39)
- 🌀 Pale blue (shade 09)
- 🌀 Petrol blue (shade 34)
- 🌀 Bright green (shade 43)
- 🌀 Orange (shade 42)
- 🌀 Bright pink (shade 44)

Tension

20 sts and 28 rows to 4in (10cm) square

Needles

1 pair 4mm (US6, UK8) needles

Other materials

- 🌀 6ft (2m) of ½in (12mm) grosgrain polka dot ribbon. We have used red but you can use any colour
- 🌀 Sewing machine or fine-pointed needle and thread in the same colour as the ribbon for making up
- 🌀 Darning needle

Cot bunting

Cast on 20 sts.
Rows 1–3: Knit.
Row 4 (decrease row): K1, k2tog, k to last 3 sts, k2tog, k1 (18 sts).
Repeat rows 1–4 until 2 sts remain.
Cast off.
Make 7 triangles.

Making up

Weave in all your ends. Sew your triangles to a length of grosgrain ribbon by hand or machine. Make two loops at each end of the ribbon for hanging up the bunting.

Wall bunting

Babies and young children will adore this chunky and vibrant bunting. String it up all year round or bring it out for birthdays and celebrations – it's a sure way to brighten up any nursery wall. Made using the same decrease style as the cot bunting on page 36, only designed to be bigger!

Yarns
Debbie Bliss Cotton DK
- Yellow (shade 35) ½ x 50g ball
- Red (shade 38) ½ x 50g ball
- Blue (shade 39) ½ x 50g ball
- Pale blue (shade 09) ½ x 50g ball
- Pale green (shade 20) ½ x 50g ball
- Bright green (shade 43) ½ x 50g ball
- Orange (shade 42) ½ x 50g ball

Tension
20 sts and 28 rows to 4in (10cm) square

Needles
1 pair 4mm (US6, UK8) needles

Other materials
- 9ft (3m) of grosgrain ribbon in a colour of your choice
- Sewing machine or fine-pointed needle and thread in the same or similar colour as the ribbon for making up
- Darning needle

Wall bunting

Cast on 40 sts.
Rows 1–3: Knit.
Row 4 (decrease row): K1, k2tog, k to last 3 sts, k2tog, k1.
Rows 5–6: Knit.
Repeat rows 4, 5 and 6 until 2 sts remain.
Cast off.
Make seven flags.

Making up
Weave in all ends. Sew your triangles to a
length of grosgrain ribbon by hand or machine.
Make two loops at each end of the ribbon
for hanging.

TOP TIP
Why not make your
bunting into a number
frieze? Cut out some felt
numbers and stick them
to your flags using fabric
glue. Or, you could spell
out baby's name in
felt letters.

Pompom scarf

This lovely button-up, scout-style scarf uses triangles, panels and delightful pompoms. It's made in an unusual L-shaped construction to give an extra snug fit around a toddler's neck. It's also secured with two bright buttons to keep them wrapped up and toasty.

Yarns
ggh Big Easy
The packaging on Big Easy indicates to use 5–6mm needles. However, for this pattern, use 4mm needles. The tension shown opposite is when used on 4mm needles.
- Blue (shade 21) ½ x 50g ball
- Pale green (shade 24) 1 x 50g ball

Tension
20 sts and 28 rows to 4in (10cm) square

Needles
1 pair 4mm (US6, UK8) needles

Other materials
- 2 x ¾in (15mm) buttons
- Darning needle

Pompom scarf

Section 1
Cast on 14 sts using pale green yarn.
Work in garter stitch for 67 rows or until work
measures 9½in (24cm).
Row 68 (buttonhole row): K3, cast off 2, k4,
cast off 2, k3.
Row 69 (buttonhole row): K3, turn work, cast
on 2, turn work, k4, turn work, cast on 2, turn
work, k3.

Shaping
Row 1 (decrease row): K1, k2tog, knit until last
3 sts, k2tog, k1 (12 sts).
Rows 2–3: Knit.
Repeat rows 1–3 until 2sts remain.
Knit a row.
Cast off.

Section 2
Cast on 14 sts.
Work in garter stitch for 48 rows or until
work measures 6¾in (17cm).

Shaping
Row 1 (decrease row): K1, k2tog, knit until
last 3 sts, k2tog, k1 (12 sts).
Rows 2–3: Knit.
Repeat rows 1–3 until 2 sts remain.
Knit a row.
Cast off.

Pompoms (make 2, using blue yarn)
Using the template below, cut out two
cardboard doughnut shapes. Place the card
pieces together and wind yarn around the
rings. Try to work clockwise around the card
to create an even pompom. You will need to
use manageable strands of yarn rather than
a ball, as this may be tricky to fit through
the central hole.

Once you have wound the yarn and have a
good coverage of your card rings, take a sharp
pair of scissors and cut the yarn around the
outer edges. Your scissor blades should pass
between the two cardboard rings. Next take
a length of yarn and pass it between the two
cardboard rings. Pull tight and tie in a double
knot. Slide the card rings off the yarn. Fluff
up your pompom and neaten any stray ends
with scissors.

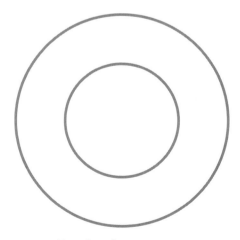

Template for pompoms
(shown at actual size)

Making up

Sew the cast-on edge of the shorter piece to the side of the longer piece using mattress stitch so the work creates an L-shape. Sew the pompoms securely to the pointed ends. Sew the buttons securely in position corresponding to the buttonholes. Weave in your ends.

TOP TIP
This pattern is suitable for a baby up to 18 months old. If you want to make a scarf for an older toddler or child, just knit an extra three or six rows in sections one and two to make them longer.

Simply stripes

Beach hut bookends

Start a nursery library with these brilliant stripey beach hut bookends. Supported with simple foam, they incorporate pebbles to give them weight. You can also knit one as a doorstop for the nursery or any room in the house.

Yarns
Rowan Handknit Cotton DK
- Red (shade 215) 1½ x 50g ball
- Pale green (shade 219) 1½ x 50g ball
- Pink (shade 313) 1½ x 50g ball
- Yellow (shade 336) ¼ x 50g ball

Tension
19–20 sts and 28 rows to 4in (10cm) square

Needles
1 pair 4mm (US6, UK8) needles

Other materials
- Foam: for the internal structure of the beach hut bookends, you will need two 6 x 6 x 4in (15 x 15 x 10cm) rectangles. For the roofs you will need two foam triangles with a 4 x 6in (10 x 15cm) base and two 2¾in (7cm) sloping sides. You can cut these from a larger piece of foam using a sharp craft knife
- Flat pebbles or stones to add weight to your bookends
- Pins for pinning your work to your foam blocks when making up
- Darning needle

Beach hut bookends

Roofs (make 4, using red yarn)
Cast on 30 sts.
Work in garter stitch for 28 rows or until work measures 4in (10cm).
Cast off.

Sides (make 2 red and 2 green)
Cast on 30 sts.
Work in garter stitch for 42 rows or until work measures 6in (15cm).
Cast off.

Bottom (make 1 red and 1 green)
Cast on 20 sts.
Work in garter stitch for 42 rows or until work measures 6in (15cm).
Cast off.

Back (make 1 green and 1 pink)
Cast on 20 sts.
Work in garter stitch for 42 rows or until work measures 6in (15cm).
Row 1 (decrease row): K1, k2tog, knit to last 3 sts, k2tog k1.
Row 2: Knit.
Repeat rows 1 and 2 until you have 2 sts left.
Knit a row.
Cast off.

Front (make 1 with pink and green stripes and 1 with green and yellow stripes)
The front panel of the beach hut is the same as the back, but after every four rows you need to change the colour of your yarn to create stripes. There is no need to tie off each time you change colour – just leave the yarn attached and pull up the next colour when you are ready to change. See page 134 for more help.

Door (make 1 pink and 1 yellow)
Cast on 20 sts.
Work in garter stitch for 14 rows or until work measures 2in (5cm).
Cast off.

> **TENSION ALERT!**
> This is a foam project, so tension matters. Refer to page 132 for instructions on working with foam.

Making up

Take your foam rectangles and, using a sharp craft knife, cut a slit in the bottom. Push a large flat stone or pebble into the slit to give your bookend some weight. Try to use a pebble that is flat so as not to warp or bulge the sides of the foam. Next, pin your knitted panels to the foam shapes and sew together using mattress stitch. Start by sewing the sides and bottom and finish with the roof, leaving a small overhang. Finally, sew your door pieces to the front of your huts.

Beach hut mobile

The bright, strong, contrasting colours in these gorgeous beach huts are designed to encourage a baby's visual development. They will cozy up any cot and they're so cute you'll want them for your own bedroom.

Yarns

ggh Big Easy
The packaging on Big Easy indicates to use 5–6mm needles. However, for this pattern, use 4mm needles. The tension shown below is when used with 4mm needles.
- Purple (shade 15) 1 x 50g ball
- Red (shade 05) 1 x 50g ball
- Blue (shade 21) 1 x 50g ball
- Pale green (shade 24) ¼ x 50g ball

Tension

20 sts and 28 rows to 4in (10cm) square

Needles

1 pair 4mm (US6, UK8) needles

Other materials

- 6ft (2m) of grosgrain ribbon in a colour of your choice
- Felt in three contrasting colours for the beach hut doors
- Fine-pointed needle and thread in colours to match the felt doors
- Foam: for the internal structure of the beach huts, you will need three 2½in (6cm) cubes of foam. For the roofs you will need three foam triangles with a 2½in (6cm) square base and two 1½ x 2½in (4 x 6cm) sloping sides. You can cut these from a larger piece of foam using a sharp craft knife
- Pins for pinning your work to the foam when making up
- Darning needle

Beach hut mobile

Bottom and sides (make 3 red, 3 blue and 3 purple)
Cast on 12 sts.
Work in garter stitch for 17 rows or until work measures 2½in (6cm).
Cast off.

Roof (make 2 red, 2 blue and 2 purple)
Cast on 12 sts.
Work in garter stitch for 12 rows until work measures 1¾in (4.5cm).
Cast off.

Back (make 1 red, 1 blue and 1 purple)
Cast on 12 sts.
Work in garter stitch for 17 rows or until work measures 2½in (6cm).
Row 1 (decrease row): K1, k2tog, knit to last 3 sts, k2tog, k1 (10 sts).
Row 2: Knit.
Repeat rows 1 and 2 until 2 sts remain.
Knit 1 row.
Cast off.

Front (make 1 with red and green stripes, 1 with blue and green stripes and 1 with purple and green stripes)
The front panel of the beach hut is the same as the back, but every two rows you need to change the colour of your yarn. There is no need to tie off each time you change colour, just leave the yarn attached and pull up when you are ready to change colour.

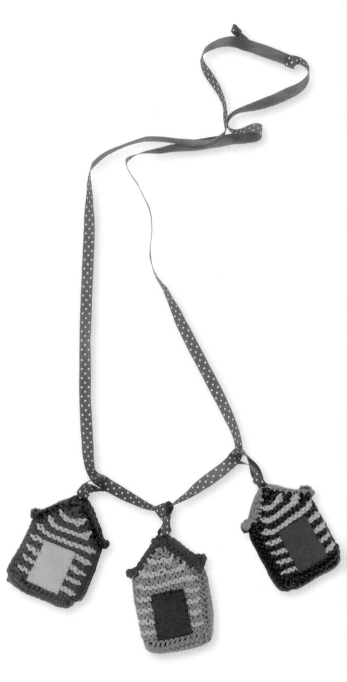

> **TENSION ALERT!**
> This is a foam project, so tension matters. Refer to page 132 for more information about working with foam.

Making up

Pin your knitted panels to the foam shapes and sew together using mattress stitch. Start by sewing the sides and bottom and finish with the roof, leaving a small overhang. Finally, cut three small doors in contrasting felt and hand stitch using straight stitch. Sew a ribbon loop to the top of each hut and string onto a longer length of ribbon.

Washing line wall hanger

These fabulous tiny tees add colourful storage above a nappy changing table or strung across a cot or bookshelves. They're perfect for baby's bits and pieces and ideal for storing your knicknacks, pegs or keys. They are made in one panel, simply folded, seamed and strung onto ribbon.

Yarns
Rowan Handknit Cotton DK
- Red (shade 215) 1 x 50g ball
- Yellow (shade 336) 1 x 50g ball
- Turquoise (shade 318) 1 x 50g ball

Jumper 1
- Yarn A – Red
- Yarn B –Yellow
- Yarn C – Turquoise

Jumper 2
- Yarn A – Yellow
- Yarn B – Red
- Yarn C – Turquoise

Jumper 3
- Yarn A – Turquoise
- Yarn B – Red
- Yarn C – Yellow

Tension
19–20 sts and 28 rows to 4in (10cm) square

Needles
1 pair 4mm (US6, UK8) needles

Other materials
- 6ft (2m) of grosgrain ribbon
- 6 x mini wooden pegs
- Darning needle

Washing line wall hanger
(make 3 – see page 54 for colourways)

Cast on 32 sts in Yarn A.

Rows 1–5: In yarn B, work in k1, p1 rib.

Row 6: In yarn C, k10, k2tog, k8, k2tog, k10 (30 sts).

Row 7: Work in garter stitch for 29 rows, changing colour so that each stripe is 10 rows wide. Cut the yarn and tie the new colour as close to the beginning of the new row as possible.

Row 36: In yarn B, knit 4 rows.

Row 40: Cast on 10 sts at start of row then knit them along with rest of row (40 sts).

Row 41 (rep row 40): Cast on 10 sts at start of row and knit (50 sts).

Rows 42–44: Knit.

Row 45: To make opening: In yarn C, k15, cast off 20, k15.

Row 46: K15, turn work and cast on 20 making sure your first cast-on stitch is tight, turn work and knit remaining 15 sts.

Rows 47–54: Knit.

Rows 55–64: In yarn B, knit.

Rows 65–74: In yarn C, knit.

Rows 75–79: In yarn B, knit.

Row 80: Cast off 10, k40.

Row 81: Cast off 10, k30.

Rows 82–84: Knit (30 sts).

Rows 85–113: In yarn C, continue in garter stitch, changing colour so that each stripe is 10 rows wide.

Row 114: K9, inc 1, k10, inc 1, k9 (32 sts).

Rows 115–119: In yarn B, work in k1, p1 rib. Cast off using Yarn A and weave in ends.

Making up

Fold your knitted jumpers in half and sew the sides and around the sleeve using mattress stitch, taking care to match up your stripes. Next, sew up the bottom of your jumpers along the upper edge of the rib so that the bottom rib edges remain open, to create the illusion of an open jumper. If you find this too tricky you can just sew along the bottom edge.

Next, using a darning needle, thread your ribbon through the jumpers, into one shoulder and out the other. Add pegs for decoration. When all three jumpers are threaded onto the ribbon, hand-sew or use a sewing machine to create loops at each end of the ribbon to hang your wall hanger.

Super stocking stitch

Loopy soother

This project combines ribbons, calico, and different textures to stimulate and comfort. A stocking stitch central panel uses purl stitch to create a smooth surface whilst a garter stitch border creates contrast.

Yarns
Debbie Bliss Cotton DK
🌀 Pale green (shade 20) 1 x 50g ball

Tension
19–20 sts and 28 rows to 4in (10cm) square

Needles
1 pair 4mm (US6, UK8) needles

Other materials
🌀 Sewing machine
🌀 25 x 3in (8cm) lengths of assorted ribbon scraps
🌀 Calico fabric
🌀 Steam iron
🌀 Darning needle

Loopy soother

Cast on 40 sts.
Rows 1–8: Knit.
Row 9: K4, p32, k4.
For purl stitch see techniques section, page 128.
Row 10: Knit.
Repeat rows 9 and 10 until work measures 7in (18cm).
Continue to work in garter stitch for 8 rows.
Cast off.

Making up

Fold your 3in (8cm) ribbon pieces in half and press with a steam iron. Machine-sew your ribbon tags to two edges of your knitted soother. Reverse the machine a few times over each ribbon for extra security. When you have attached your ribbons, press your soother flat and measure the edges.

TOP TIP
Make two identical soothers so that you can wash them without the baby noticing!

Adding an extra ⅜in (1cm) around the edges for your hem, use those measurements to cut a piece of calico cotton for your soother back. Next, iron the hem of the calico flat and sew it to the back of the knitted soother, ensuring all the ribbon ends are concealed.

Sail-away boat tidy

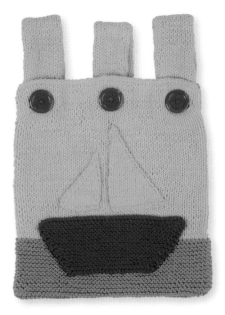

Keep clutter under control with our lovely 1950s-inspired tidy. Three strong ties attach the tidy to the side of a cot or changing table. It's robust, practical and will entertain a baby's imagination – where can the mice be sailing away to?

Yarns
Rowan Handknit Cotton DK
- Light blue (shade 327) 2 x 50g ball
- Dark blue (shade 335) 1 x 50g ball
- Red (shade 215) oddments
- Yellow (shade 336) oddments

Tension
19–20 sts and 28 rows to 4in (10cm) square

Needles
1 pair 4mm (US6, UK8) needles

Other materials
- Three 1½in (3cm) diameter buttons of your choice
- Darning needle

Sail-away boat tidy

Boat
Cast on 40 sts.
Rows 1–3: Knit.
Row 4 (decrease row): K1, k2tog, k to last 3 stitches, k2tog, k1 (38 sts).
Row 5–6: Knit.
Repeat rows 4–6 until 24 sts remain.
Repeat row 4 (22 sts) (total of 28 rows).
Cast off.

Large sail
Cast on 15 sts.
Row 1: Purl (see techniques section, page 128).
Row 2 (decrease row): K1, k2tog, k to end of row.
Repeat rows 1–2 until 3 stitches remain (24 rows).
Row 25: Purl.
Row 26: K1, k2tog.
Row 27: K2tog, tie off.

Small sail
Cast on 10 sts.
Row 1: Purl.
Row 2 (decrease row): Knit to last 3 sts, k2tog, k1
Repeat rows 1–2 until 3 sts remain (14 rows).
Row 19: Purl.
Row 20: K1, k2tog.
Row 21: K2tog, tie off.

Front panel (sea and sky)
Cast on 50 sts.
Rows 1–30: Knit.
Row 31: Change colour to pale blue for sky. Starting with a k row, work in stocking stitch for 50 rows.
Buttonhole row: On the next purl row, p4, cast off 4, p15, cast off 4, p15, cast off 4, p4.
Next row: K4, turn work around and cast on 4, turn work and k15, turn work, cast on 4, turn work and k15, turn work and cast on 4, turn work and k4.
Continue in stocking stitch for a further 8 rows (total of 90 rows).
Cast off.

Back panel
Begin by measuring the front panel.
Cast on 50 sts.
Knit in garter stitch until the back panel is the same length of the front panel (approx 90 rows).

Cot ties (make 3)
Cast on 12 sts.
Knit for 120 rows or until work measures 16in (40cm).
Cast off.

Mouse
For mouse pattern see page 92.

Making up

Front panel
Pin front panel to a cushion with the smooth stocking stitch side facing you. Position boat and sails, pin and put a few quick tacking stitches to hold in place. Then sew boat and sails on securely using a darning needle and simple overstitch. (See page 136 for technical help.)

Back panel
Place front and back panels together with right sides facing outwards. Sew together using mattress stitch. (See page 136 for technical help.)

Cot ties
Fold ties in half and sew edges together using mattress stitch. Sew a button on to one end. With button side facing away from you, sew the non-button end to the back panel.

Junior jumper

This super cute sailor's jumper is designed for comfort with an easy on and off open boat neck. Bringing together stocking stitch, decreases and funky stripes, it's easy to make and a great way to buck the trend for baby pink and blue. Make a bold statement and choose your own mix of vibrant colours.

Yarns
Rowan Handknit Cotton DK
- Red (shade 215) 2–2½ x 50g balls
- Green (shade 219) 2–2½ x 50g balls

Tension
19–20 sts and 28 rows to 4in (10cm) square

Needles
1 pair 4mm (US6, UK8) needles

Other materials
- Darning needle

Sizes
0–3[3–6:6–9:9–12] months

TOP TIP
If you are knitting for a baby born in the spring or summer, they will have grown by winter time – so think ahead and plan a larger size.

Junior jumper

Sleeves (make these first)

Cast on using the red yarn 30[32:34:36] sts.

Rows 1–4: Knit.

Row 5 (increase row): K7, inc1, k to last 7 sts, inc1. 32[34:36:38] sts.

Change colour of yarn now and every 4 rows thereafter to create stripes. There is no need to tie and cut off your yarns as you change colour; just carry the yarn up the side of the work.

Rows 6–10: Starting with a purl row, work in stocking stitch.

Row 11 (increase row): K2, inc1, k to last 3 sts, inc1, k2.

Continue to work in stocking stitch and increase on every sixth row as above until you have 40[44:48:52] sts.

Work in stocking stitch for a further 12[6:7:2] rows. You should be at the end of a green stripe. Now change the colour of your yarn to begin a red stripe – this is crucial to making sure the stripes on the body and sleeve match when you sew them up.

Decrease rows: P2, p2tog, p to last 4 sts, p2tog, p2.

Continue to work in stocking stitch, decreasing every row as before, until you have 6 sts left.
K1, k2tog, k2tog, k1 (4 sts).
K2tog, k2tog (2 sts).
Cast off.

Back and front

Cast on using the red yarn 43[47:51:55] sts.

Rows 1–4: Knit.

Row 5 (increase row): K10, inc1, work to final 10 sts, inc1, k to end. 45[49:53:57] sts.

Change colour of yarn now and alternate every 4 rows thereafter to create stripes.

Starting with a purl row, work in stocking stitch for the next 44[52:60:68] rows. You should now be at the end of a green stripe.

Change yarn for next row. This should be red. This is crucial for making sure your stripes match on the body and sleeves of your jumper.

Decrease rows: K1, k2tog, work to final 3 sts, k2tog, k1. 43[47:51:55] sts. N.B. Depending on which size jumper you are making, you may find this decrease row falls on a purl row, in which case substitute k2, k2tog for p2, p2tog etc.

Continue to work in stocking stitch and decrease on every fifth row until 37[41:43:47] sts remain.

Work in stocking stitch for a further 1[3:0:0] rows.
Work in garter stitch for 2 rows.
Cast off.

> **TENSION ALERT!**
> Tension matters for this pattern as it will affect the size of your finished garment. You could make a larger or smaller size if you have tight or loose tension. See techniques section, page 132 for more help.

Making up

Use a hot steam iron to press your sections flat. (Do not use a hot iron if you swapped our suggested cotton DK for a yarn containing wool or acrylic.)

Using mattress stitch (see technical chapter on page 136 for help), sew the shoulders of the front and back sections together. Then sew the open sleeves to the front and back. Finally, sew the sides of the jumper into the armpits and along the length of the sleeves. Weave in your ends.

Creative increases

Draughty dog

Our sausage dog will become an old friend and family heirloom. We designed it to keep out draughts along the door but it can also be used as a floor cushion or a much loved toy. Perfect for a nursery, it will also cozy up any room in the house! Make it as long or as short as you like by adapting the stripes along the body.

Yarns

Rowan Handknit Cotton DK

- Red (shade 215)
  1 x 50g ball
- Turquoise (shade 318)
  1 x 50g ball
- Green (shade 219)
  ½ x 50g ball
- Pink (shade 313)
  ½ x 50g ball
- Purple (shade 334)
  ½ x 50g ball
- Orange (shade 337)
  ½ x 50g ball
- Oddments of Dark Blue
  (shade 277) for features

Tension

19–20 sts and 28 rows
to 4in (10cm) square

Needles

1 pair 4mm (US6, UK8) needles

Other materials

- 1 x 9oz (250g) bag of
  child-safe toy stuffing
- Felt circles for eyes
  (2 for each eye)
  2 x approx ¾in (2cm)
  diameter
  2 x approx 1in (2.5cm)
  diameter
- Darning needle

Draughty dog
(starting at tail end)

Cast on 20 sts.
Row 1: Knit.
Row 2: Purl.
Row 3 (increase row): *k2, inc 1, repeat from * 5 more times, k2 (26 sts).
Row 4: Purl.
Row 5 (increase row): *k2, inc 1, repeat from * 7 more times, k2 (34 sts).
Row 6: Purl.
Row 7 (increase row): K8, inc 1, k3, inc 1, k3, inc 1, k3, inc 1, k9 (39 sts).
Row 8: Purl.
Row 9: K10, inc 1, k3, inc 1, k3, inc 1, k1, inc 1, k3, inc 1, k3, inc 1, k10 (45 sts).
Row 10: Purl.
Row 11: *k4, inc 1, repeat from * to end 8 more times (54 sts).
Row 12: Purl.

Row 13: Change colour and, starting with a knit row, continue in stocking stitch, changing colour after every 15 rows to create 8 stripes, ending on a purl row.

Shaping the head
Change colour now.
Rows 1–12: Starting with a knit row, work in stocking stitch for 12 rows, ending on a purl row.
Row 13: K4, k2tog, k14, inc 1, k4, inc 1, k2, inc 1, k4, inc 1, k14, k2tog, k4 (56 sts).
Row 14: Purl.
Row 15: K4, k2tog, k14, inc 1, k4, inc 1, k4, inc 1, k4, inc 1, k14, k2tog, k4 (58 sts).
Row 16: Purl.
Row 17: K4, k2tog, k14, inc 1, k4, inc 1, k6, inc 1, k4, inc 1, k14, k2tog, k4 (60 sts).
Row 18: Purl.

Change colour now.
Row 19: K4, k2tog, k19, inc 1, k8, inc 1, k19, k2tog, k4 (60 sts).
Rows 20–26: Starting with a purl row, continue in stocking stitch for 7 rows.
Row 27: K19, k2tog, k3, k2tog, k8, k2tog, k3, k2tog, k19 (56 sts).
Row 28: Purl.
Row 29: K19, k2tog, k3, k2tog, k4, k2tog, k3, k2tog, k19 (52 sts).
Row 30: Purl.
Row 31: K18, k2tog, k3, k2tog, k2, k2tog, k3, k2tog, k18 (48 sts).
Row 32: Purl.
Row 33: K4, k2tog, k13, k2tog, k6, k2tog, k13, k2tog, k4 (44 sts).
Row 34: Purl.
Change colour now.

TOP TIP
Use your sausage
dog as a floor bumper
cushion: curl him around
to create back support
for a baby learning
to sit up.

Row 35: K4, k2tog, k32, k2tog, k4 (42 sts).
Row 36: Purl.
Row 37: K4, k2tog, k4, k2tog, k4, k2tog, k6, k2tog, k4, k2tog, k4, k2tog, k4 (36 sts).
Row 38: Purl.
Row 39: K4, k2tog, k7, k2tog, k6, k2tog, k7, k2tog, k4 (32 sts).
Row 40: Purl.
Row 41: K4, k2tog, k20, k2tog, k4 (30 sts).
Row 42: Purl.
Change colour now.
Row 43: K4, k2tog, k4, k2tog, k6, k2tog, k4, k2tog, k4 (26 sts).
Row 44: Purl.
Row 45: Knit.

Row 46: Purl.
Row 47: K4, k2tog, k14, k2tog, k4 (24 sts).
Row 48: Purl.
Row 49: Knit.
Row 50: Purl.
Change colour now.
Row 51: Knit.
Row 52: Purl.
Row 53: Knit.
Row 54: Purl.
Row 55: K3, k2tog, k3, k2tog, k4, k2tog, k3, k2tog, k3 (20 sts).
Row 56: Purl.
Row 57: K1, k2tog, k3, k2tog, k4, k2tog, k3, k2tog, k1 (16 sts).
Cast off purlwise.

Outer ears (make two)

Cast on 10 sts.
Row 1: Purl.
Row 2 (increase row): K1, inc 1, knit to last two sts, inc 1, k1 (12 sts).
Row 3: Purl.
Rows 4–5: Rep rows 2 and 3 (14 sts).
Row 6: Rep row 2 (16 sts).
Rows 7–17: Starting with a purl row, continue in stocking stitch.
Row 18 (decrease row): K1, k2tog, knit to last 3 sts, k2tog, k1 (14 sts).
Row 19: Purl.
Row 20: Knit.
Row 21: Purl.
Row 22 (decrease row): K1, k2tog, knit to last 3 sts, k2tog, k1 (12 sts).
Rows 23–30: Rep rows 19–22 until 8 sts remain.
Cast off purlwise.

Inner ears (make 2)

Cast on 9 sts.
Row 1: Purl.
Row 2 (increase row): K1, inc 1, knit to last 2 sts, inc 1, k1 (11 sts).
Row 3: Purl.
Rows 4–5: Rep rows 2 and 3 (13 sts).

Row 6: Rep row 2 (15 sts).
Rows 7–17: Starting with a purl row, continue in stocking stitch.
Row 18 (decrease row): K1, k2tog, knit to last 3 sts, k2tog, k1 (13 sts).
Row 19: Purl.
Row 20: Knit.
Row 21: Purl.
Row 22 (decrease row): K1, k2tog, knit to last 3 sts, k2tog, k1 (11 sts).
Rows 23–26: Rep rows 19–22 until 9 sts remain.
Cast off purlwise.

Feet (make 4)

Cast on 14 sts.
Rows 1–12: Starting with a knit row, work in stocking stitch, changing colour after every fourth row.
Row 13: Change colour and cast on 6 sts, knit cast on sts and rest of row (20 sts).

Row 14: Cast on 6 and pearl both the cast on sts and rest of row (26 sts).
Row 15: K1, inc 1, k11 , inc 1, k10, inc1, k1 (29 sts).
Row 16: Purl.
Row 17: K1, inc 1, k 12, inc 1, k12, inc 1, k1 (32 sts).
Row 18: Purl.
Row 19: K1, k2tog, k 10, k2tog, k2, k2tog, k10, k2tog, k1 (28 sts).
Row 20: Purl.
Row 21: K2tog and repeat to end of row (14 sts).
Row 22: Purl.
Cast off.

Tail

Cast on 16 sts.
Row 1: Knit.
Row 2: Purl.
Continue in stocking stitch for a further 8 rows.

Row 11: Change colour and work in stocking stitch for 10 rows.
Row 21: Change colour and knit.
Row 22: Purl.
Row 23: K7, k2tog, k7 (15 sts).
Row 24: Purl.
Row 25: Knit.
Row 26: Purl.
Row 27: K7, k2tog, k6 (14 sts).
Row 28: Purl.
Row 29: Knit.
Row 30: Purl.
Row 31: Change colour and knit.
Row 32: Purl.
Row 33: K6, k2tog, k6 (13 sts).
Row 34: Purl.
Row 35: Knit.
Row 36: Purl.
Row 37: K6, k2tog, k5 (12 sts).
Row 38: Purl.
Row 39: Knit.
Row 40: Purl.

Rows 41–42: Change colour and rep rows 39–40.
Row 43: K5, k2tog, k5 (11 sts).
Row 44: Purl.
Row 45: Knit.
Row 46: Purl.
Row 47: K5, k2tog, k4 (10 sts).
Rows 48–50: Rep rows 38–40.
Row 51: Change colour, knit.
Row 52: Purl.
Row 53: K4, k2tog, k4 (9 sts).
Row 54: Purl.
Row 55: K4, k2tog, k3 (8 sts).
Row 56: Purl.
Row 57: K3, k2tog, k3 (7 sts).
Row 58: Purl.
Row 59: K3, k2tog, k2 (6 sts).
Row 60: Purl.
Row 61: K2tog 3 times (3 sts).
Cast off purlwise.

Making up

Use a hot steam iron to press your sections flat. (Do not use a hot iron if you substituted cotton yarn for wool or acrylic.) Using mattress stitch, start at the nose end and sew the body seam with WS together and RS facing outward. Stuff with toy stuffing to shape as you go. Sew up the feet starting with the toe end. Stuff with toy stuffing and shape before sewing shut. Sew the tail in the

same way. Pin the two sides of the ears together (the inner ear should sit inside the outer ear) and sew together with yarn in the colour of your outer ear. Sew ears, legs and tail to the body and secure with a knot. Weave ends into the body.

Features

Using a contrasting colour, sew on a nose using overstitch and mouth features using backstitch. Cut out two circles in different coloured felt – approx ¾in (2cm) and 1in (2.5cm) in diameter. Secure the two pieces together using a French knot, then sew them securely to the dog's face using small overstitches. Tie off securely with a knot and weave in thread ends.

Pompom pixie hat

Inspired by a 1950s design, this adorable pompom hat uses simple increases and decreases to unique effect – it's easy to make, fun to wear and will keep a baby cozy and warm all year round!

Yarns
ggh Big Easy
The packaging on Big Easy indicates to use 5–6mm needles. However, for this pattern, use 4mm needles. The tension shown below is when used with 4mm needles.
🌀 Pale green (shade 24) 1–1½ x 50g ball
🌀 Blue (shade 21) ½ x 50g ball

Tension
20 sts and 28 rows to 4in (10cm) square

Needles
1 pair 4mm (US6, UK8) needles

Sizes
0–3 [3–6:6–9:9–12] months

Other materials
🌀 Pompom maker – see page 42 for template
🌀 1 x ⅝in (15mm) button

TENSION ALERT!
Tension matters for this pattern as it will affect the size of your finished garment. Rather than trying to adapt the pattern, we suggest you opt for making a larger or smaller size if you have tight or loose tension. (See techniques section, page 132 for more help.)

Pompom pixie hat

Cast on 24 [26:28:30] sts.
Rows 1–8: Knit.
To make a larger size than 0–3, knit a further 3:6:9 rows and continue the pattern as follows.
Row 9 (increase row): K1, 1nc1, k2 last 2 sts, inc1, k1. 26[28:30:32] sts.
Rows 10–17: Knit.
Row 18: Rep row 9. 28[30:32:34] sts.
Rows 19–26: Knit.
Row 27: Rep row 9. 30[32:34:36] sts.
Row 28 (wrong side): K to last 2 sts, inc 1, k1. 31[33:35:37] sts.
Row 29 (right side): K1, inc1, k to end. 32[34:36:38] sts.
Rep rows 28 and 29 until 36[38:40:42] sts.
Row 34 (wrong side): Knit.
Row 35 (right side): Cast on 3 sts, knit to end. 39[41:43:45] sts.
Row 36: Knit.
Repeat rows 35 and 36 until 48[50:52:54] sts.
Rows 42–48: Knit.
Row 49 (right side): Cast off 3 sts, k to end. 45[47:49:51] sts.
Row 50: Knit.
Repeat rows 49 and 50 until 36[38:40:42] sts remain.
Row 56 (wrong side): Knit.
Row 57 (right side): K2, k2tog, k to end. 35[37:39:41] sts.
Row 58: K to last 3 sts, k2tog, k1. 34[36:38:40] sts.
Repeat rows 57 and 58 until 30[32:34:36] sts remain.
Row 63 (wrong side): K1, k2tog, k2 last 3 sts, k2tog, k1. 28[30:32:34] sts.
Rows 64–72: Knit.

Row 73: K1, k2tog, k2 last 3 sts, k2tog, k1. 26[28:30:32] sts.
Rows 74–81: Knit.
Row 82: K1, k2tog, k2 last 3 sts, k2tog, k1. 24[26:28:30] sts.
Rows 83–90: Knit.
To make a larger size than 0–3, knit a further 3:6:9 rows before casting off.
Cast off.

Strap

Cast on 6 sts.
Rows 1–5: Knit.
Row 6 (buttonhole row): K2, cast off 2, k2.
Row 7: K2, turn work, cast on 2, ensuring that you pull the yarn very tight as you cast on. Turn work back, k2.
Continue to work in garter stitch until work measures 5[5¼:5½:5¾]in (13[13.5:14:14.5]cm).
Cast off.

Pompom

Using the templates on page 42, cut out two cardboard doughnut shapes. Place the card pieces together and wind yarn around the rings. Work clockwise around the card using lengths of yarn rather than a ball, as this may be tricky to fit through the central hole. Once you have good coverage of your card rings, take a sharp pair of scissors and cut the yarn around the edges. The blades should pass between the two cardboard rings. Take a length of yarn and pass it between the two cardboard rings. Pull tight and tie in a double knot. Slide the card rings off the yarn. Fluff up your pompom and neaten any stray ends with scissors.

Making up

Using mattress stitch, sew up the back seam of the hat. Attach the pompom. Next sew the chin strap to the hat and secure the button using a needle and cotton thread.

TOP TIP
For more coziness, make the scarf to match this hat, on page 40.

Juicy apple rattle

Our juicy apple comes complete with its own chomping caterpillar! Inside is a home-made rattle so it couldn't be easier. It is an ideal first toy – easy to grasp, textured, squeezable and fun to shake. The apple is made in one piece ending at the stalk with the leaf and caterpillar added separately.

Yarns
Debbie Bliss Cotton DK
🌀 Red (shade 38) ½ x 50g ball
🌀 Bright green (shade 43) ¼ x 50g ball
🌀 Orange (shade 42) oddments
🌀 Yellow (shade 35) oddments

Tension
20 sts and 28 rows to 4in (10cm) square

Needles
1 pair 4mm (US6, UK8) needles

Other materials
🌀 Toy stuffing
🌀 Empty lip salve pot
🌀 Dried beans to create rattle
🌀 Darning needle

Juicy apple rattle

Apple body
Cast on 5 sts.
Row 1: Purl.
Row 2 (increase row): K1, inc1, k1, inc1, k1 (7 sts).
Row 3: Purl.
Row 4 (increase row): K1, *inc1, rep from * to end of row (13 sts).
Row 5: Purl.
Row 6 (increase row): K1, *inc, rep from * until the end of the row (25 sts).
Row 7: Purl.
Row 8 (increase row): K1, *inc1, k2, rep from * until end of the row (33 sts).
Row 9: Purl.
Row 10 (increase row): K1, *inc1, k3 rep from * until end of the row (41 sts).
Row 11: Purl.
Row 12 (increase row): K1, *inc1, k4 rep from * until end of the row (49 sts).
Row 13: Purl.
Row 14 (increase row): K1, *inc1, k5 rep from * until end of the row (57 sts).
Rows 15–23: Continue to work in stocking stitch, ending on a purl row.
Row 24 (decrease row): K1, * k2tog, k5, rep from * until end of the row (49 sts).

Row 25: Purl.
Row 26 (decrease row): K1, * k2tog, k4, rep from * until end of the row (41 sts).
Row 27: Purl.
Row 28 (decrease row): K1, * k2tog, k3, rep from * until end of the row (33 sts).
Row 29: Purl.
Row 30 (decrease row): K1, * k2tog, k2, rep from * until end of the row (25 sts).
Row 31: Purl.
Row 32 (decrease row): K1, *k2tog, rep from * until end of the row (13 sts).
Row 33: Purl.
Row 34 (decrease row): K1, *k2tog, rep from * until end of the row (7 sts).
Row 35: Purl.
Change yarn to green.
Row 36 (decrease row): K1, k2tog, k1, k2tog, k1 (5 sts).
Row 37: Purl.
Row 38 (decrease row): K2tog, k1, K2tog (3 sts).
Rows 39–43: Starting with a purl row, work in stocking stitch. Cut your yarn and thread it through the remaining 3 sts and sew up the seam of the apple stalk.

Leaves (make 2)
Cast on 2 sts.
Row 1: Knit.
Row 2 (increase row): Inc1, inc1 (4 sts).
Row 3: K1, p2, k1.
Row 4: Knit.
Row 5: K1, p2, k1.
Row 6 (increase row): Inc1, k2, inc1 (6 sts).
Row 7: K2, p2, k2.
Row 8 (increase row): Inc1, k4, inc1 (8 sts).
Row 9: K3, p2, k3.
Row 10: Knit.
Row 11: K3, p2, k3.
Row 12: Knit.
Row 13: K3, p2, k3
Row 14 (decrease row): K2tog, k4, k2tog (6 sts).
Row 15: K2, p2, k2.
Row 16 (decrease row): K2tog, k2, k2tog (4 sts).
Row 17: K1, p2, k1.
Row 18 (decrease row): K2tog, k2tog (2 sts).
Cast off.

Caterpillar
Cast on 3 sts using yellow yarn. Work in stocking stitch, alternating yarn colour every 2 rows to create stripes. Continue until you have 7 stripes.
Cast off.

Making up

Starting at the stalk end, sew up the apple
seam using mattress stitch. When you are
2in (5cm) from completing the seam, stuff
the apple firmly with toy stuffing, placing your
empty lip salve or cosmetics pot containing
dried beans in the centre. Finish off the seam
and weave in your ends. Next, firmly sew your
two leaves to the base of the stalk and weave
in the ends. Finally, sew along the seam of your
caterpillar and attach it to your apple.

Interactive toys

Munching mice and cheese

This fantastic toy creates a fun game to play with a baby – our hungry mice are attached to their delicious cheese with Velcro. They are small enough for little hands to enjoy pulling them off and reattaching them in new arrangements. You can also knit these cute mice to sail away in the boat tidy on page 62.

Yarns

Rowan Handknit Cotton DK
- Red (shade 215) oddments
- Pink (shade 313) oddments
- Yellow (shade 336) 1 x 50g ball
- Oddments of any yarn for the features

Tension

19–20 sts and 28 rows to 4in (10cm) square

Needles

1 pair 4mm (US6, UK8) needles

Other materials

- Sewable Velcro (yellow)
- Fine-pointed needle for sewing on Velcro
- Toy stuffing
- Yellow cotton thread
- A wedge shape of fire-resistant foam, height 4in (10cm) x width 4in (10cm) x length 6in (15cm), cut diagonally
- Darning needle

Munching mice

Mouse body

Cast on 8 sts.

Row 1: Purl.

Row 2: *K1, inc1, rep from * until end of row (12 sts).

Row 3: Purl.

Row 4: *K1, inc1, rep from * until end of row (18 sts).

Work in stocking stitch for 8 rows.

Row 13: *k1, k2tog, rep from * until end of row (12 sts).

Row 14: Purl.

Row 15: K3, k2tog, k2, k2tog, k3 (10 sts).

Row 16: Purl.

Row 17: K2, k2tog, k2, k2tog, k2 (8 sts).

Row 18: Purl.

Row 19: K2tog 4 times (4 sts).

Cast off.

Mouse ears

Cast on 5 sts.

Knit 5 rows.

Cast off.

Making up

Body

Start at the nose and, using mattress stitch, sew the cast-off edge together, then continue along the body seam. Stuff with child-safe toy stuffing before closing the back end and tying off. Leave a long thread of wool for a tail.

Features

For eyes, sew French knots (see techniques section, page 137). Thread the yarn through the nose for whiskers. Pinch the ears and sew in position. Make sure all the thread is knotted and secured safely. Sew on Velcro very securely along the bottom seam for interactivity with the cheese.

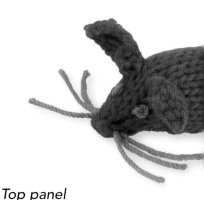

Cheese

Base
Cast on 20 sts.
Work in garter stitch for
42 rows or until your work
measures 6in (15cm).
Cast off.

End panel
This end of the cheese is the
size of a tension square but
involves creating texture by
alternating knit and purl
stitches.
Cast on 20 sts.
Row 1: K12, p3, k5.
Row 2: Knit.
Row 3: K11, p5, k4.
Row 4: Knit.

Row 5: K10, p7, k3.
Row 6: Knit.
Row 7: K3, p3, k5, p5, k4.
Row 8: Knit.
Row 9: K2, p5, k5, p3, k5.
Row 10: Knit.
Row 11: K2, p5, k13.
Row 12: Knit.
Row 13: K3, p3, k14.
Rows 14–16: Knit.
Row 17: K10, p1, k9.
Row 18: Knit.
Row 19: K9, p3, k8.
Row 20: Knit.
Row 21: K10, p1, k9.
Continue to work in garter
stitch for 7 rows or until work
measures 4in (10cm).

Top panel
Cast on 20 sts.
Rows 1–2: Knit.
Row 3: K 13, p1, k6.
**Row 4 and all even-
numbered rows:** Knit.
Row 5: K12, p3, k5.
Row 7: K6, p3, k4, p1, k6.
Row 9: K5, p5, k10.
Row 11: K5, p5, k10.
Row 13: K6, p3, k11.
Row 15: Knit.
Row 17: K3, p1, k16.
Row 19: K2, p3, k15.
Row 21: K3, p1, k16.
Row 23: Knit.
Row 25: K9, p3, k8.
Row 27: K8, p5, k7.
Row 29: K8, p5, k7.
Row 31: K9, p3, k8.
Row 33: Knit.
Row 35: K4, p3, k13.
Row 37: K3, p5, k12.
Row 39: K4, p3, k4, p3, k6.
Row 41: K10, p5, k5.
Row 43: K10, p5, k5.
Row 45: K4, p1, k6, p3, k6.
Row 47: K3, p3, k14.
Row 49: K3, p3, k14.
Row 51: K4, p1, k15.
Cast off or continue in
garter stitch until your
work measures 7in (18cm).

TENSION ALERT!
You need to measure your tension
with your chosen yarn before starting
this project to work out how many
stitches you need to match the foam
measurements. OR you can knit the
cheese panels and get the foam
cut to your own specification
after you've completed your
knitting and measured it.
See page 132 for
additional help.

Side panel 1
Cast on 20 sts.
Row 1: Knit.
Row 2 (decrease row): K1, k2tog, k to end (19 sts). Repeat rows 1 and 2 three times (16 sts).
Row 9: K3, p3, k10.
Row 10: Rep row 2 (15 sts).
Row 11: K2, p5, k8.
Row 12: Rep row 2 (14 sts).
Row 13: K2, p5, k7.
Row 14: Rep row 2 (13 sts).
Row 15: K3, p3, k7.
Row 16: Rep row 2 (12 sts).
Rows 17–18: Knit.
Row 19: K until last 3 stitches, k2tog, k1 (11 sts).
Rows 20–22: Knit.
Row 23: Rep row 19 (10 sts).
Row 24 and even-numbered rows 26–38: Knit.
Row 25: Rep row 19 (9 sts).
Row 27: Rep row 19 (8 sts).
Row 29: Rep row 19 (7 sts).
Row 31: Knit.
Row 33: Rep row 19 (6 sts).
Row 35: Knit.
Row 37: Rep row 19 (5 sts).
Row 39: K1, k2tog, k2 (4 sts).
Row 40: K1, k2tog, k1 (3 sts).
Row 41: K1, k2tog (2 sts).
Row 42: K2tog.
Tie off.

Side panel 2
Cast on 20 sts.
Row 1 and odd-numbered rows 3–19: Knit.
Row 2: K1, k2tog, k10, p3, k4 (19 sts).
Row 4: K1, k2tog, k8, p5, k3 (18 sts).
Row 6: K1, k2tog, k7, p5, k3 (17 sts).
Row 8: K1, k2tog, k7, p3, k4 (16 sts).
Row 10: K1, k2tog, k13 (15 sts).
Row 12: K1, k2tog, k12 (14 sts).
Row 14: K1, k2tog, k11 (13 sts).
Row 16: K1, k2tog, k10 (12 sts).
Row 18: K1, k2tog, k9 (11 sts).
Row 20: Knit.
Row 21: K until last 3 stitches, k2tog, k1 (10 sts).
Rows 22–23: Knit.
Row 24: K1, k2tog, k4, p1, k2 (9 sts).
Row 25: Knit.
Row 26: K1, k2tog, k2, p3, k1 (8 sts).
Row 27: Knit.
Row 28: K4, p3, k1 (8 sts).
Row 29: K to last 3, k2tog, k1 (7 sts).
Row 30: K4, p1, k2.
Row 31: K to last 3, k2tog, k1 (6 sts).
Row 32: K1, k2tog, k3 (5 sts).
Rows 33–35: Knit.
Row 36: K2, k2tog, k1 (4 sts).
Rows 37–38: Knit.
Row 39: K1, k2tog, k1 (3 sts).
Row 40: Knit.
Row 41: K1, k2tog.
Row 42: K2 tog.
Tie off.

Making up
Pin the pieces to your foam. Sew the top, end and bottom panels together using mattress stitch. Pin the side panels in place and sew. Weave in your ends. Sew on Velcro dots (use corresponding side of the Velcro used for the mice).

Cosmic cube

An adorable activity-packed intergalactic cube that uses texture, colour and shape to encourage play and exploration. Satisfying to make, each side features a different activity to create a space-themed storytelling focus for imaginary tales of adventure.

Yarns
Debbie Bliss Cotton DK
- Pale blue (shade 09) 2 x 50g balls
- Blue (shade 39) 2 x 50g balls
- Red (shade 38) 1 x 50g ball
- Bright green (shade 43) 2 x 50g balls
- Yellow (shade 35) ¼ x 50g ball

Tension
20 sts and 28 rows to 4in (10cm) square

Needles
1 pair 4mm (US6, UK8) needles

Other materials
To construct the interior of the cube you will need the following pieces of foam:
- Two 8 x 8 x 4in (20 x 20 x 10cm) pieces of foam (when these pieces are placed together they should form a cube shape)
- Darning needle
- Craft knife to cut out your alien bunker
- Sewable Velcro
- Felt
- 3 x ½in (13mm) buttons
- 3 x 1½in (4cm) buttons
- 1 x large clown button
- Stitch holder or safety pin
- 1 x 6in (15cm) square plastic mirror tile
- Set square
- Foam or furniture glue

Cosmic cube

Base

Section A (make 2)
Cast on 20 sts using red yarn.
Work in garter stitch for 28 rows or until work measures 4in (10cm).
Cast off.

Section B (make 1)
Cast on 20 sts using green yarn.
Work in moss stitch for 28 rows or until work measures 4in (10cm).
Cast off.

Section C (make 1)
Cast on 20 sts using green yarn.
Work in rib for 28 rows or until work measures 4in (10cm).
Cast off.

Sides (make 2)
Cast on 40 sts using pale blue yarn.
Work in garter stitch for 56 rows or until work measures 8in (20cm).
Cast off.

Secret alien bunker (make 5)
Cast on 18 sts using green yarn.
Work in garter stitch for 26 rows or until work measures 3½in (9cm).
Cast off.

Bunker trap door (make 1)
Cast on 26 sts using green yarn.
Rows 1–5: Knit.
Row 6: Purl.
Row 7: Knit.
Row 8: Purl.
Rows 9–15: Knit.
Repeat rows 6–15 until work measures 5in (12.5cm).
Buttonhole row: K5, cast off 2, k5, cast off 2, k5, cast off 2, k5.
Buttonhole row: K5, turn work, cast on 2, turn work, k5, turn work, cast on 2, turn work, k5, turn work, cast on 2, turn work, k5.
Continue to work in garter stitch for 7 rows.
Cast off.

Moon sides (make 2)
Cast on 40 sts using yellow yarn.
Rows 1–13: Knit
Change colour to dark blue yarn. Starting with a purl row, work in stocking stitch until work measures 8in (20cm).
Cast off.

TENSION ALERT!
Tension matters for this project, as you don't want your cube cover to be baggy around your foam. Tight tension will work, but if you have loose tension, always deduct a stitch or two when casting on or have the cube cut to your specification after you've finished your knitting and measured it accurately. See the tension section on page 132 for more help.

Top (make 1)

Cast on 40 sts using red yarn. Work in garter stitch until work measures 2in (5cm), ending on a wrong side row.

Right side row: K11, cast off 18, k11. Place 11 sts on stitch holder.

Work the remaining 11 sts in garter stitch until work measures 3.5in (9cm). Place stitches onto stitch holder. Cut yarn, leaving a tail.

Connect yarn to other 11 sts and work in garter stitch until work measures 3.5in (9cm). At end of final row, cast on 18 sts.

Turn work.

Take other stitches off holder, tie tail to ball of yarn and knit to end (40 sts).

Work in garter stitch for further 2in (5cm).

Cast off.

Rocket pocket (make 1)

Cast on 15 sts using red yarn. Work in garter stitch until work measures 4in (10cm). Cast off.

Rocket top (make 1)

Cast on 16 sts using orange yarn.

Rows 1–3: Knit.

Row 4 (decrease row): K1, k2tog to last 3, k2tog, k1 (14 sts).

Row 5: Knit.

Row 6: Rep row 4 (12 sts).

Row 7: Knit.

Row 8: Rep row 4 (10 sts).

Row 9: Knit.

Row 10: Rep row 4 (8 sts).

Row 11: Knit.

Row 12: Rep row 4 (6 sts).

Row 13: Knit.

Row 14: K1, k2tog, k2tog, k1 (4 sts).

Row 15: Knit.

Row 16: K2tog, k2tog (2 sts).

Row 17: K2tog.

Cast off.

Mirror frame (make 1)

Cast on 28 sts using red yarn. Work in garter stitch until work measures 1¼in (3cm).

Next row: K6, cast off 16, k6. Continue to work in garter stitch along one side of the frame (6 sts) until work measures 3in (8cm). Cut yarn and place on stitch holder.

Tie yarn to your other 6 stitches and continue to work in garter stitch until work measures 3in (8cm).

At end of last row, cast on 16 stitches.

Turn work and k6.

Next row: Knit (28 sts). Continue to work in garter stitch for a further 1¼in (3cm). Cast off.

Button ups (make 1 red, 1 yellow, 1 green)

Cast on 20 sts.
Rows 1–6: Knit.
Row 7 (buttonhole row): K4, cast off 4, k to end.
Row 8 (buttonhole row): K up to buttonhole, turn the work and cast on 4 sts, ensuring that you pull the yarn very tight as you cast on. Turn the work back and k to end. (For additional technical help with buttonholes, see page 131.)
Rows 9–14: Knit.
Cast off.

Cutting your foam

Before you start making up your cube you will need to cut away a section from the centre of each of your foam pieces to create your alien bunker.

Using a set square and a marker pen, draw these measurements onto the foam:
3½ x 3½ x 1¾in (9 x 9 x 4.5cm) – see image A.

Next, using a sharp craft knife, cut out the sections – see image B. When you place your two foam pieces together you should have a 3½in (9cm) cube-shaped bunker hole. Don't worry if your sides look a bit rough – all this will be concealed when you sew the cube up. Once you have cut your bunker recess, use foam or furniture glue to stick the two pieces together.

Find out how to make the aliens that sit in the alien bunker on page 106.

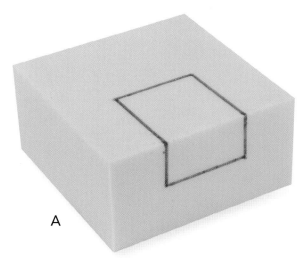

A

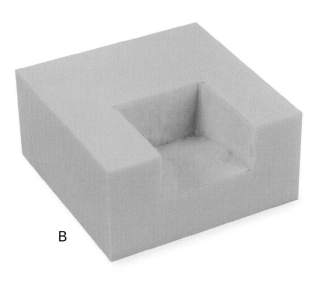

B

Making up

Sew your four bottom squares together to make a larger square and pin to the bottom of your cube. Next, pin your four sides to your cube and sew all seams using mattress stitch. Finally, pin your top section and sew it to the side panels.

Alien bunker: Take your five squares and sew together to create a cube shape. Place your cube shape into your foam recess to line the walls. Next sew the top seams of your alien bunker to the corresponding seams on the top of your cube. Finally, attach your trap door and buttons.

Templates for felt stars

Templates for felt planets

Templates for felt rocket fins

cut this slit

cut this slit

cut this slit

Template for rings around planets

Once your cube is made up you can start adding your embellishments.

Mirror: Using foam glue, glue your plastic mirror tile securely to the side of your cube. Next, take your knitted mirror frame and sew to your cube around the edge of the mirror tile using mattress stitch. Finally, use a little bit of glue to attach the edges of the mirror tile to the inside of your knitted frame.

Rocket pocket and button ups: Attach the knitted pieces to the sides of your cube using mattress stitch (see page 136). Add the buttons, making sure that you secure them well.

Felt: Using templates on page 103, cut out your felt stars, planets and rocket fins. Using a fine needle, attach the felt decorations to your cube using straight stitch.

SAFETY ALERT!
Because the cosmic cube contains small parts, children under three should be supervised whilst at play.

Alien friends

Add a surprise to your cosmic cube with these cute, cuddly alien friends. They are quick to knit, so make as many as you like in strong colours to bring your cosmic cube to life. Made in two sections, each side is identical with only one simple seam to sew.

Yarns
Debbie Bliss Cotton DK
- Orange (shade 42) ⅓ x 50g ball
- Bright green (shade 43) ⅓ x 50g ball
- Yellow (shade 35) ⅓ x 50g ball
- Oddment of black or navy yarn for features

Tension
20 sts and 28 rows to 4in (10cm) square

Needles
1 pair 4mm (US6, UK8) needles

Other materials
- Felt for eyes
- Toy stuffing
- Stitch holder or safety pin
- Darning needle

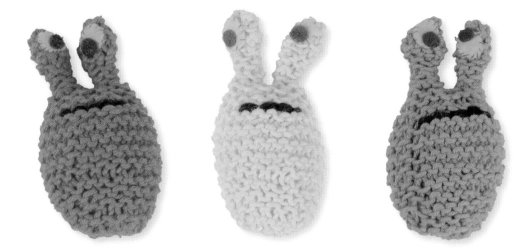

Alien friends
(make 2 in yellow, 2 in orange and 2 in green)

Cast on 5 sts.
Row 1: Knit.
Row 2 (increase row): K1, inc1, k1, inc1, k1 (7 sts).
Rows 3–4: Knit.
Row 5 (increase row): K2, inc1, k1, inc1, k2 (9 sts).
Rows 6–7: Knit.
Row 8 (increase row): K3, inc1, k1, inc1, k3 (11 sts).
Rows 9–10: Knit.
Row 11 (increase row): K4, inc1, k1, inc1, k4 (13 sts).
Rows 12–17: Knit.
Row 18 (decrease row): K4, k2tog, k1, k2tog, k4 (11 sts).
Row 19: Knit.
Row 20 (decrease row): K3, k2tog, k1, k2tog, k3 (9 sts).
Row 21: Knit.
Row 22 (decrease row): K2, k2tog, k1, k2tog, k2 (7 sts).

Row 23: Knit.
Row 24 (decrease row): Cast off 1, k2, cast off 1, k3 (5 sts).
Row 25 (decrease row): Cast off 1, k2, place remaining 2 stitches on a stitch holder.
Rows 26–31: Work your 2 stitches in garter stitch for 6 rows.
Row 32 (increase row): Inc1, inc1 (4 sts).
Rows 33–35: Knit.
Row 36 (decrease row): K2tog, k2tog (2 sts). Cast off.
Cut your yarn, leaving a tail for sewing up. Next, remove your 2 stitches from the stitch holder and reattach your yarn. Work in garter stitch for 6 rows.
Next row (increase row): Inc1, inc1 (4 sts).
Next row: Work in garter stitch for 3 rows.
Decrease row: K2tog, k2tog (2 sts). Cast off.

Making up

Place the two sections of your alien body together, wrong sides facing. Sew along the seam from the bottom up towards the eye stalks, using mattress stitch. Continue around the eyes and back down the side, leaving the bottom of the alien open. Stuff firmly with toy stuffing and close the bottom seam. Weave in your ends. Next, cut two small felt ovals and two felt circles in colours of your choice. Sew to the eye stalks using a fine needle and contrasting cotton thread. Cut a small piece of Velcro and attach to the back of one of your aliens. Sew another piece of Velcro to the side of the cube.

Bunny buddy

Float off to the land of Zzzzzzzzzzz with this gorgeous bedtime bunny. So huggable, it's the perfect gift for any child or even for yourself! Designed with bedtime in mind, it'll keep a child company as they float off to sleep. Constructed in simple sections, this simple knit is a lot easier to create than it looks.

Yarn
Debbie Bliss Cotton DK
- Pale blue (shade 09) 2 x 50g balls
- Red (shade 38) 1 x 50g ball
- Oddments of yarn for features

Tension
20 sts and 28 rows to 4in (10cm) square

Needles
1 pair 4mm (US6, UK8) needles

Other materials
- Toy stuffing
- Darning needle

Bunny buddy

Head

Cast on 30 sts using main colour.

Row 1: Purl.

Row 2 (increase row): K1, inc1, knit to last two sts, inc1, k1 (32 sts).

Row 3: Purl.

Row 4 (increase row): K1, inc1, k14 to middle, inc1, k13 to last two sts, inc1, k1 (35 sts).

Row 5: Purl.

Row 6 (increase row): K1, inc1, k15, inc1, knit 15 to last 2 sts, inc1, k1 (38 sts).

Row 7: Purl.

Row 8 (increase row): K1, inc1, k16 to middle, inc1, inc1, knit 16 to last 2 sts, inc1, k1 (42 sts).

Row 9: Purl.

Row 10 (increase row): K1, inc1, k19 to middle, inc1, k18 to last 2 sts, inc1, k1 (45 sts).

Row 11: Purl.

Row 12 (decrease row): K1, k2tog, knit to last 3 sts, k2tog, k1 (43 sts).

Row 13: Purl.

Row 14 (decrease row): Rep row 12 (41 sts).

Row 15 (decrease row): P1, p2tog, purl to last 3 sts, p2tog, p1 (39 sts).

Row 16 (decrease row): Rep row 12 (37 sts).

Row 17 (decrease row): Rep row 15 (35 sts).

Row 18 (decrease row): Rep row 12 (33 sts).

Row 19 (decrease row): Rep row 15 (31 sts).

Row 20 (decrease row): K1, k2tog, k11 to middle 2 sts, k2tog, k12 to last 3 sts, k2tog, k1 (28 sts).

Row 21 (decrease row): P1, p2tog, p10 to middle 2 sts, p2tog, purl to last 3 sts, p2tog, p1 (25 sts).

Row 22 (decrease row): K1, k2tog, k6, k2tog, k2, k2tog, k7, k2tog, k1 (21 sts).

Row 23 (decrease row): P1, p2tog, p7, p2tog, p6 to last 3 sts, p2tog, p1 (18 sts).

Row 24 (decrease row): K2tog right across row (9 sts).

Row 25 (decrease row): P2tog, p2tog, p1, p2tog, p2tog (5 sts).

Using a darning needle, thread the yarn through the remaining stitches and gather together.

Outer ears (make 2)

Cast on 15 sts using main colour.

Rows 1–14: Starting with a knit row, work in stocking stitch.

Row 15: K6, k2tog, k7 (14 sts).

Row 16: Purl.

Row 17: K6, k2tog, k6 (13 sts).

Row 18: Purl.

Row 19: K5, k2tog, k6 (12 sts).

Row 20: Purl.

Row 21: K5, k2tog, k5 (11 sts).

Row 22: Purl.

Row 23: K4, k2tog, k5 (10 sts).

Row 24: Purl.

Row 25: K4, k2tog, k4 (9 sts).

Row 26: Purl.

Row 27: K3, k2tog, k4 (8 sts).

Row 28: Purl.

Row 29: K3, k2tog, k3 (7 sts).

Row 30: Purl.

Row 31: K2, k2tog, k3 (6 sts).

Row 32: Purl.

Row 33: K2, k2tog, k2 (5 sts).

Row 34: Purl.

Row 35: K1, k2tog, k2 (4 sts).

Row 36: Purl.

Row 37: K1, k2tog, k1 (3 sts). Cast off.

Inner ears (make 2)

Cast on 14 sts using contrasting colour.

Rows 1–13: Starting with a purl row, work in stocking stitch.

Row 14: K6, k2tog, k6 (13 sts).

Row 15: Purl.

Row 16: K5, k2tog, k6 (12 sts).

Row 17: Purl.

Row 18: K5, k2tog, k5 (11 sts).

Row 19: Purl.
Row 20: K4, k2tog, k5 (10 sts).
Row 21: Purl.
Row 22: K4, k2tog, k4 (9 sts).
Row 23: Purl.
Row 24: K3, k2tog, k4 (8 sts).
Row 25: Purl.
Row 26: K3, k2tog, k3 (7 sts).
Row 27: Purl.
Row 28: K2, k2tog, k3 (6 sts).
Row 29: Purl.
Row 30: K2, k2tog, k2 (5 sts).
Row 31: Purl.
Row 32: K1, k2tog, k2 (4 sts).
Row 33: Purl.
Row 34: K1, k2tog, k1 (3 sts).
Row 35: Purl.
Row 36: K1, k2tog (2 sts).
Cast off.

Body

Cast on 20 sts in main colour.
Row 1: Knit.
Row 2: Purl.
Row 3: *k4, inc1, rep from *
3 more times until end of row
(24 sts).
Row 4: Purl.
Row 5: Knit.
Row 6: Purl.
Row 7: *k5, inc 1, rep from *
3 more times (28 sts).
Rows 8–10: Rep rows 4–6.
Row 11: Knit.
Row 12: Purl.
Row 13: *k6, inc1, rep from *
3 more times (32 sts).
Rows 14–16: Rep rows 4–6.
Row 17: *k7, inc1, rep from *
3 more times (36 sts).
Rows 18–20: Rep rows 4–6.
Row 21: Knit.
Row 22: Purl.
Row 23: *k8, inc1, rep from *
3 more times (40 sts).
Row 24–26: Rep rows 4–6.
Row 27: *k9, inc1, rep 3 more
times (44 sts).
Rows 28–30: Rep rows 4–6.
Row 31: K1, k2tog, k9, k2tog,
k9, k2tog, k9, k2tog, k8 (40 sts).
Row 32: P7, p2tog, p8, p2tog,
p8, p2tog, p8, p2tog, p1 (36 sts).
Row 33: K1, k2tog, k7, k2tog,
k7, k2tog, k7, k2tog, k6 (32 sts).
Row 34: P5, p2tog, p6, p2tog,
p6, p2tog, p6, p2tog, p1
(28 sts).
Row 35: K1, k2tog, k5, k2tog,
k5, k2tog, k5, k2tog, k4 (24 sts).
Row 36: P3, p2tog, p4, p2tog,
p4, p2tog, p4, p2tog, p1 (20 sts).
Row 37: K1, k2tog, k3, k2tog,
k3, k2tog, k3, k2tog, k2 (16 sts).
Row 38: P1, p2tog, p2, p2tog,
p2, p2tog, p2, p2tog, p1 (12 sts).
Row 39: K1, k2tog, k1, k2tog,
k1, k2tog, k1, k2tog (8 sts).
Using a darning needle,
thread the yarn through the
remaining stitches and gather
together.

Arms (make 2)

Cast on 10 sts using pale blue
yarn.
Row 1: Knit.
Row 2: Purl.
Rows 3–30: Change colour
and knit. Continue in stocking
stitch, changing colour every
2 rows.

Shaping the paw

Row 31: In contrast colour
*k1, inc 1, rep from * to end
of row (15 sts).
Row 32: Purl.
Row 33: *k1, inc1, rep from *
to last stitch, k1 (22 sts).
Row 34: Purl.
Row 35: *k1, inc 1, rep from
* to end (33 sts).
Row 36: Purl.
Row 37: K1, *k2tog, rep from
* to end (17 sts).
Row 38: Purl.
Row 39: K1, *k2tog, rep from
* to end (9 sts).
Draw thread through remaining
stitches and pull to gather.

Legs (make 2)

Cast on 10 sts using pale blue yarn.

Row 1: Knit.

Row 2: Purl.

Rows 3–50: Change colour and knit. Continue in stocking stitch, changing colour every 2 rows. After 50 rows, make foot as follows:

Row 51: In contrast colour, *k1, inc 1, rep from * to end of row (15 sts).

Row 52: Purl.

Row 53: *K1, inc 1, rep from * to last stitch, k1 (22 sts).

Row 54: Purl.

Row 55: *K1, inc 1, rep from * to end (33 sts).

Row 56: Purl.

Row 57: *K1, k2tog, rep from * to end (17 sts).

Row 58: Purl.

Row 59: *K1, k2tog, rep from * to end (9 sts).

Draw thread through remaining stitches and pull to gather together.

Making up

Body

Starting from the gathered stitches at the base, with right sides facing outwards, use mattress stitch to sew the side of the body together, leaving the neck open. Stuff with toy stuffing.

Head

Fold in half with right sides facing outwards. Starting at the nose use mattress stitch to sew along the brow and chin, stopping at the cast-on edge to stuff the head with toy stuffing. Continue to sew the cast-on edge of the head to the cast-on edge of the body, joining the head and body together to make the neck. Make sure that there is enough stuffing in the neck to support the head. Weave in your ends. For the bunny's features, create the eyes and mouth using backstitch and add eyelashes and a nose using overstitch. For technical help on stitches see page 136.

Ears

Pin inner ears to outer ears with right sides facing outwards so the inner ear sits inside the outer ear. Sew together with simple running stitch using a strand of your main colour to match the outer ear.

Arms and legs

Starting with the gathered stitches at the toes and paws, use mattress stitch to sew along the seam, filling with toy stuffing as you go. Attach arms to the 'shoulders' near the neck. Attach legs to the front edge of the body so that the bunny can sit on its bottom with the legs falling forward.

TOP TIP
As you are sewing up the body, slip in a lavender sachet to help baby drift off to sleep.

Bunny dress

Dress the bunny each morning in this cute little dress. Knitted from the hem up, it uses garter, stocking and moss stitch to create a pinafore. The main dress has only one seam and simply slips over the bunny's body.

Yarns
Debbie Bliss Cotton DK
- Pink (shade 44) ½ x 50g ball
- Oddment of a contrasting colour for bow detail

Tension
20 sts and 28 rows to 4in (10cm) square

Needles
1 pair 4mm (US6, UK8) needles

Other materials
- Stitch holder or safety pin
- Darning needle

Bunny dress

Cast on 60 sts.
Rows 1–3: Knit.
Row 4: Purl.
Row 5: Knit.
Row 6: Purl.
Row 7: Knit.
Row 8: Purl.
Row 9: K1, k2tog, *k8, k2tog, rep from * 4 times until last 7 sts, k7 (54 sts).
Row 10: Purl.
Row 11: K1, k2tog, *k7, k2tog, rep from * 4 times until last 6 sts, k6 (48 sts).
Row 12: Purl.
Row 13: K1, k2tog, *k6, k2tog, rep from * 4 times until last 5 sts, k5 (42 sts).
Row 14: Purl.
Row 15: K1, k2tog, *k5, k2tog, rep from * 4 times until last 4 sts, k4 (36 sts).
Row 16: Purl.
Row 17: K2tog, k2tog, *k4, k2tog, rep from * 4 more times, k2tog (28 sts).
Row 18: Purl.
Row 19: Knit.
Row 20: Knit 14 sts and place remaining sts on a safety pin. Turn the work.
Row 21 (moss stitch first row): *k1, p1, rep from * to end of row (14 sts).
Row 22 (moss stitch second row): * P1, k1, rep from * to end of row.
Rows 23–24: Rep rows 21–22.
Rows 25–26: Rep rows 21–22.
Row 27: *k1, p1, rep from * to end
Row 28: K2tog, p1, k1, cast off 6 (using appropriate k and p sts so your last cast-off st is a knit), p1, k1, p2tog.
Row 29: P1, k1, p1, turn the work.
Rows 30–37: Rep row 29.
Cast off 3 sts, tie off and cut yarn leaving a long tail. Turn the work.
Row 38: Reattach yarn to the 3 sts still on the needle: k1, p1, k1.
Rows 39–46: Rep row 38.
Cast off 3 stitches, tie off and cut the yarn leaving a long tail.
Take the remaining 14 stitches off the stitch holder or safety pin and place them onto a needle so that you are ready to knit with the wrong side facing you (the bumpy side is the 'wrong side').
Row 47: Reattach yarn to the first stitch and with the WS facing, knit the 14 sts.
Row 48 (moss stitch first row): *k1, p1, rep from * to end of row (14).
Row 49 (moss stitch second row): * P1, k1, rep from * to end of row.
Rows 50–51: Rep rows 48–49.
Rows 52–53: Rep rows 48–49.
Rows 54–55: Rep rows 48–49.
Cast off.

Making up

Using mattress stitch, start at the bottom hem of the dress (the cast-on edge) and sew the two sides together, taking care that both sides match up. Stop once you reach the moss stitch sections and tie off the yarn to leave the armhole. Lay the dress flat with the two moss stitch panels together, fold over the shoulder straps and stitch them in place to complete the yoke of the dress. Weave in the ends. Next, thread a darning needle with a double strand of contrasting yarn and, using running stitch, weave it in and out of the 'waist'. Knot securely before tying into a bow.

Bunny jumper

Give your bunny a change of clothes or keep it warm in winter with this little cozy knit jumper. It's so quick and easy you could make several in brilliant unisex colours, or even try one in stripes!

Yarn
Debbie Bliss Cotton DK
🌀 Green (shade 43) ½ x 50g ball

Tension
20 sts and 28 rows to 4in (10cm) square

Needles
1 pair 4mm (US6, UK8) needles

Other materials
🌀 Darning needle

Bunny jumper

Body panel (make 2)
Cast on 24 sts.
Rows 1–2: Knit.
Row 3: Purl.
Rows 4–6: Starting with a purl row, work in stocking stitch.
Row 7: K1, k2tog, knit until 3 sts remain, k2tog, k1 (22 sts).
Rows 8–10: Starting with a purl row work in stocking stitch.
Row 11: Cast on 7 sts and knit (29 sts).
Row 12: Cast on 7 sts and purl (36 sts).

Rows 13–23: Starting with a knit row, work in stocking stitch.
Row 24: Cast off 10 sts and knit rest of row (26 sts).
Row 25: Cast off 10 sts and purl rest of row (16 sts).
Row 26: Purl.
Row 27: Knit.
Cast off.

Making up
Lay the cast-off edges of the body panels together with right sides facing outwards. Using mattress stitch, sew the cast-off edges together just at the shoulders and arms, leaving the bulk of this seam open for the head. Next, start at the cast-on edge of the body panels and sew up the remaining seams along the body and arm. Weave in any ends.

TOP TIP
Why not use colours
that match your
Junior jumper
(see page 66) for
a matching
bunny outfit?

Techniques

Getting started

Basic materials

This book is designed so you can start with a minimum of equipment. Where patterns require additional items these are listed with the individual patterns.

Must haves:

- One set of knitting needles size 4mm (US6, UK8)
- One large, blunt darning needle for sewing up
- Scissors
- Ruler
- Pins

Casting on

1 Create a loop on the left-hand needle secured with a slip knot. This will count as your first stitch.

2 Hold the needle with the loop in your left hand. Take the other needle in your right hand and insert the tip through the loop from front to back. Wrap the yarn anti-clockwise around the right-hand needle.

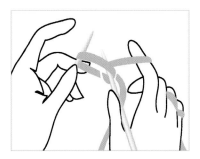

3 Use the right hand needle to draw the yarn under and through to create a new loop.

4 Slip this new loop of yarn onto the left-hand needle. You have now cast on your second stitch. Repeat steps 2–4 until you have got the number of stitches stated in the pattern.

Casting off

1 Knit the first two stitches of the row, then, using the left-hand needle, pass the first stitch over the top of the second stitch and off the needle entirely. This stitch will now lay flat around the neck of your second stitch.

2 Knit the next stitch, then, using the left-hand needle, pass the second stitch over and off the needle. Repeat to the end of the row until one stitch remains. Cut the yarn leaving a long tail, thread the tail through the last stitch and pull tight to tie off.

Stitches

Knit stitch

1 With stitches on the left-hand needle, take the other needle in your right hand and insert it into the first loop from front to back (away from you) and through the left side to the right side of the loop. Take the free yarn and pull it around the right-hand needle from the back to the front in an anti-clockwise direction.

2 Use the right-hand needle to pull this yarn under and through the loop.

3 With this new loop still on the right-hand needle, push the rest of that stitch off the left-hand needle. Repeat until you have completed the row, then turn the work and repeat from step 1.

Purl stitch

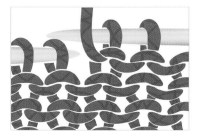

1 With the yarn to the front of the work, insert the right-hand needle into the first loop on the left-hand needle, from the back towards the front of the loop and right to left (the exact opposite direction to a knit stitch).

2 Pass the free yarn around the right-hand needle in an anti-clockwise direction.

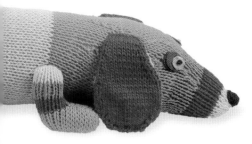

Stitch patterns

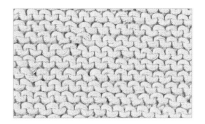

Garter stitch
This is the simplest pattern and involves knitting rows of knit stitch only, creating a textured, elastic surface.

Stocking stitch
Stocking stitch is made of alternating rows of knit stitch and purl stitches. This creates one side with a smooth texture, as the stitches line up with rows of 'v' shapes (this is called the 'right side', or RS) and the other side is textured (the 'wrong side', or WS).

3 Use the right-hand needle to pull the yarn through the loop (away from you). Keeping this loop on the right-hand needle, slip the rest of the stitch off the left-hand needle. Repeat until the end of the row.

Single rib
Rib involves alternating knit and purl stitch. After a knit stitch, the yarn is moved forward between the needles, ready for the purl stitch and vice versa. This creates vertical stripes of texture that are very elastic.

Moss stitch
Moss stitch is similar to rib, using alternating knit and purl stitches, but they are 'offset' so that, for an even number of stitches, the first row will start with a knit, then a purl but the second row will start with a purl, then a knit. This creates an attractive, alternating raised pattern.

Shaping

Increasing

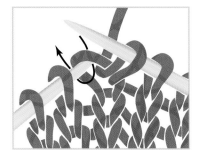

1 Knit into the stitch as if you are creating a normal stitch, but do not slip the stitch off the left-hand needle.

2 Re-insert the right-hand needle, from front to back, into the back of the stitch and knit the stitch as normal, slipping both parts of the stitch off the left-hand needle onto the right-hand needle.

Decreasing

1 Insert your needle from front to back through the first two stitches on the left-hand needle at the same time.

2 Knit one stitch just as if you were completing any normal knit stitch. Purling two stitches together on a purl row achieves the same effect.

ON INCREASING
Once you have increased into a stitch, that stitch has been counted in the pattern. Where you see 'k1, inc1, k7' you should k1, then increase into the next stitch, then go on to knit a further seven stitches.

Making buttonholes

Buttonholes are made by casting off stitches in the middle of a row. Then, in the next row, turn the work and cast those stitches back on, then turn the work and carry on with the row. This creates a slit. Make sure your first cast-on stitch is tight to keep your knitting neat.

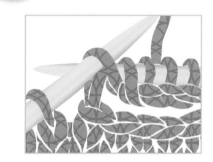

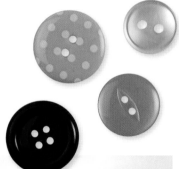

Tension

What is tension?

Tension is how tightly or loosely you knit your stitches. Like handwriting, your particular tension is unique to you.

Does tension matter?

Tension only matters with certain projects in this book. For example, if you are making the apple rattle on page 84 it doesn't really matter if your apple comes out larger or smaller than the one in the picture. But if you spend hours making the jumper on page 66, only to find that your tension is very tight and you end up with a jumper that's too small, you'll be none too pleased. To make life easier, we've put tension alert boxes with all the patterns that require you to think about tension.

Your tension

Before you start making a 'tension alert' project, you need to check your tension. You do this by knitting a tension square. Using your 4mm (US6, UK8) needles and cotton DK yarn, cast on 20 stitches and work in garter stitch for 28 rows. Cast off. Next, lay the square flat and measure the width of the square. If it measures 4in (10cm) then your tension is perfect. However, you may find it measures less than 4in (10cm) – this means you have tight tension. If your work measures more than 4in (10cm), you have loose tension. Likewise with the length of the work – you may find it takes you more or less than 28 rows to reach a 4in (10cm) length.

Fixing tension problems

Tight tension
For the foam projects in this book, tight tension is not a problem, as your knitting will stretch nicely over the foam. If you are making a piece of clothing such as the pixie hat on page 80, then we suggest making the next size up from the one you need to prevent your item turning out on the small side.

Loose tension
If you are making a clothing item, then we suggest making a size smaller than you need If you have loose tension, you have two choices when making foam items. You can knit up your pieces without adapting the pattern and have your foam cut to the right size once finished. For example, if you make up the panels for the ABC blocks on page 22 and find that they come up 4½ x 4½in (11 x 11cm), not 4 x 4in (10 x 10cm) as the pattern states, then you can just get a foam cube cut to that size.

Or better still, you can adapt the pattern to suit your tension. Adapting patterns is actually much simpler than you think and in many ways easier than getting your foam cut to the size of your knitting. Measure the width of your tension square to work out how loose your tension is. Next, you need to adapt the pattern by deducting stitches when you cast on.

When casting on, each stitch adds approx. ¼in (5mm) to the width of your work. So in order to make your work narrower, you need to deduct stitches when casting on. For example, if your tension square width measures 4½in (11cm), you need to deduct two stitches when casting on (cast on 18 where the pattern says 20 and so on) and you will lose ½in (1cm) from the width of your work.

Useful know-how

Creating stripes

To start a new stripe, simply cut your yarn and attach a new colour of yarn by knotting very close to the edge of the row. In your new colour, continue knitting. When you want to change colour again, repeat. Once you finish your knitting you will be left with stray ends where you have changed colours. This is fine for items like Bunny buddy on page 110 and Draughty dog on page 72, where the stray ends will be concealed once your work is sewn up.

However, for narrow stripes of four or two rows, like the jumper on page 66, you can try carrying your yarns up the side of your work rather than cutting and tying off each time you change colour. This method only works on stripes with even rows.

Using foam

Using non-toxic furniture foam is an alternative to toy stuffing and an easy way to create cute items with crisp edges. If it's new to you, don't be daunted – let your local furniture foam supplier do the hard work and pre-order it cut to the specific size. You'll find some details of foam suppliers on page 141.

For patterns using foam, tension is really important because you want your knitting to fit snugly over the foam. See our tension section on page 132 for more information about tension and foam.

Whilst most of the projects in this book use foam that has been pre-cut, there are a couple of items that will require you to cut the foam yourself to create shapes. Instructions for these are found within the individual patterns.

Be sure to take time to measure correctly and use a sharp craft knife. Don't worry if your edges appear rough – they will all be concealed inside your knitting when you come to make up the object.

Non-toxic furniture foam

Sewing up

Mattress stitch

Sewing up correctly with mattress stitch keeps seams invisible and gives your item a neat finish. Place the pieces to be sewn side-by-side on a flat surface (it helps to press them with a steam iron if possible), with the right side facing towards you. Secure a thread to the work and bring the needle up between the first and second stitch of one piece. Find the corresponding stitch in the second piece and, taking the thread over the top of the work, take the needle underneath the horizontal part of the second stitch from the edge.

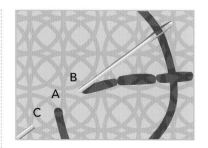

Backstitch

Working from right to left, bring the needle up to the right side of the work at point A, down at point B and back up at point C. Try to keep the distance between A, B and C even. The next stitch begins at point C, which is the new point A.

Running stitch

This is the simplest sewing stitch. Bring the needle up through the fabric and back down again a small distance away, then up and down again, keeping the space between the stitches as even as possible.

Straight stitch

This simple stitch is used to sew felt to knitting. Insert the needle so the thread comes up in the interior of the felt shape around ¼in (5mm) from the edge. Insert the needle back into the knitting at the same spot but underneath the felt. This will make the stitch fall neatly at 90 degrees to the felt edge, then bring the needle and thread up again a little way along.

Finishing touches

French knots

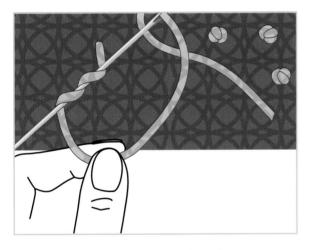

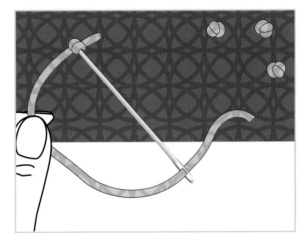

1 Bring the needle and thread up from the bottom to the top (right side) of the fabric. Hold the thread taut with the left hand and use the right hand to wind the needle around that thread.

2 Hold the thread taut and insert the needle close to the place where it came out, pulling the needle down through the fabric. Keep some tension on the thread with your left hand as you pull through, feeding the thread through the twists that are left behind.

Troubleshooting

Extra stitches

A common mistake is to gain stitches – they can mysteriously appear in your knitting! This is often because a stitch hasn't been completed properly by being slid off the left-hand needle. It's worth taking your knitting off the needle and undoing it until you find the fault (this is called 'frogging') and carefully knitting up the row again.

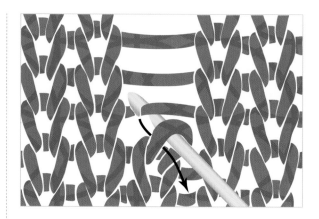

Loose stitches

If you find you have loose stitches at the sides of your work, it can sometimes help to slip the first stitch onto the right-hand needle without knitting it and then knit straight into the second stitch. This leaves a neater edge.

Dropped stitches

If stitches slip off the ends of your needles, they can ladder. The most important thing is to 'catch' the stitch to stop it laddering further. You can either undo your knitting to that point and knit it carefully again or else you can thread the loop up through the knitting using a crochet hook (shown above). Hold your knitting with the right side facing you, 'catch' the stitch that has dropped and pick up the next horizontal bar. Then pass the horizontal bar through the stitch. Repeat as necessary.

Abbreviations

Approx	approximately
Cm	centimetres
Cont	continue
DK	double knitting
Foll	following
In(s)	inch(es)
Inc	increase by working twice into stitch
K	knit
K2tog	knit two stitches together
P	purl
P2tog	purl two stitches together
Rem	remaining
Rep	repeat
RS	right side of work
St(s)	stitch(es)
WS	wrong side of work
*	work instructions following * then repeat as directed
( )	repeat instructions inside brackets as directed
[ ]	shows increments of sizes

Conversions

Knitting needle conversions

UK	Metric	US
14	2mm	0
13	2.5mm	1
12	2.75mm	2
11	3mm	–
10	3.25mm	3
–	3.5mm	4
9	3.75mm	5
8	4mm	6
7	4.5mm	7
6	5mm	8
5	5.5mm	9
4	6mm	10
3	6.5mm	10.5
2	7mm	10.5
1	7.5mm	11
0	8mm	11
00	9mm	13
000	10mm	15

UK/US yarn weights

UK	US
4–ply	Sport
Double knitting	Light worsted
Aran	Fisherman/worsted
Chunky	Bulky
Super chunky	Extra bulky

Suppliers

Yarns

We have used Debbie Bliss Cotton DK, Rowan Handknit Cotton and ggh Big Easy, but you can supplement these yarns for any cotton DK or sport-weight yarn.

Debbie Bliss
UK:
www.norfolkyarn.co.uk
Independently run shop and online store
www.laughinghens.com
An online knitting and crochet treasure trove
www.angelyarns.com
UK-based store with shipping worldwide
US:
www.theknittinggarden.com
Online store and boutique
www.ebay.com
Online auction site
Australia:
www.thewoolshack.com
Shop and online store with extensive range
For worldwide stockists visit:
www.debbieblissonline.com

Rowan
UK:
www.johnlewis.com
Branches throughout the UK
www.angelyarns.com
Europe's largest online yarn store with worldwide shipping
US:
www.purlsoho.com
New York-based yarn boutique and online store
www.hamptonknittingyarn.com
Wide range available online
Australia:
www.sunspun.com.au
Well-stocked online store
For worldwide stockists visit:
www.knitrowan.com

ggh
UK:
www.loop.gb.com
Gorgeous knitting boutique and online store
US:
www.muenchyarns.com
Distributor of ggh in the US
For worldwide stockists visit:
www.ggh-garn.de

Other materials

Most of the additional materials in this book can be bought at any good haberdashery shop. We also source many crafty bits and pieces online at the auction site, Ebay.

Ribbon
UK:
www.vvrouleaux.com
Specialist shop and online store

Foam
Look in your local directory for foam suppliers in your area, or use an online store who supply foam cut to order.
UK:
www.efoam.co.uk
www.twfoam.co.uk
US:
www.foamorder.com
Australia:
www.foamsales.com.au

Acknowledgments

AUTHORS' ACKNOWLEDGEMENTS
Without the help of some very special people this book would not have been possible. Huge thanks go to Lyn Atkinson, Penny Batchelor, Eileen Edmunds, Annie Moseley, Ruth Whippman and Barbara Roberts for their precious time and hardworking hands. We really couldn't have done it without you! To Paula Gilder for her dangerous speed-knitting and for her meticulous eye. To Gareth and Colin for their patience and tea making. To Buster for pattern inspiration and testing. To Katrin our pattern checker for keeping us on the straight and narrow, and to Gerrie Purcell and Virginia Brehaut at GMC for their help, guidance and above all, for giving us this opportunity to publish our designs.

PUBLISHER'S ACKNOWLEDGEMENTS
Child photography by Chris Gloag
Still life photography by Rebecca Mothersole
Flat photography by Anthony Bailey
Illustrations by Simon Rodway
Pattern checking by Katrin Salyers

GMC Publications would like to thank the following babies, toddlers and their mummies and daddies for allowing us to photograph them for this book:
Faith, Jacob, Josef, Vermilion and Zac.

GMC Publications would also like to thank the following shops in Lewes, East Sussex for allowing us to take photographs in them:
Bags of Books, Brats, Flint and Lewes Antiques Centre.

Index

To place an order, or to request a catalogue, contact:
GMC Publications, Castle Place, 166 High Street,
Lewes, East Sussex BN7 1XU United Kingdom
Tel: +44 (0)1273 488005 Fax: +44 (0)1273 402866
www.gmcbooks.com